THE STONE FIDDLE

To my mother
Brigid Tunney
with whom it all began

PADDY TUNNEY

THE STONE FIDDLE

My Way to Traditional Song
with an introduction by
BENEDICT KIELY

To Bob.

with kindest regards.

And as the cobbler
Raked the fire
and held once more
the flat-toed tongs
He sought the Land of
Hearts' Desire
And lingered with The
Man of Songs

GILBERT DALTON   DUBLIN   — Paddy Tunney

First published in 1979 by
GILBERT DALTON LTD.
SHENICK ROAD
SKERRIES
CO. DUBLIN

Copyright ©, 1979, Paddy Tunney

Cover and motif by Steven Hope

The publisher acknowledges the
assistance of the Arts Council of
Northern Ireland in the
publishing of this volume

Set in Press Roman type by
Joe Healy Typesetting, Dublin
Printed in Ireland by
Genprint Ltd, Dublin

CONTENTS

Paddy Tunney tells herein, and among many other stories, the story of the stone fiddle of Castlecaldwell and of Denis McCabe the fiddler who was drowned in the waters of the Erne: so it is less than necessary for me to repeat it here. Yet it has always seemed to me that the stone fiddle stands by the Erne shore as a significant and influential symbol in the heart of a district particularly rich in song, music, poetry and legend. This book proves to me that my belief was well justified: it will prove the same to the many who will find in its pages the original delight that I have found.

In that district the family of the man who writes this book was particularly distinguished. Indeed in a story of my own, written some years ago, I acknowledged and honoured that truth by having an old man say about a holiday journey: "A pity in a way we didn't make as far as the stone fiddle. We might have heard good music. It's a curious thing that in the townlands around that place the people have always been famed for music and singing. The Tunneys of Castlecaldwell now are noted. It could be that the magic of the stone fiddle has something to do with it."

Paddy Tunney as he grew up was very much aware of the stone fiddle and his telling of the history of that odd monument moves off into a splendid Gothic fantasy of the re-appearance of the drowned Denis McCabe in the company of the ghost of Carolan, the harper, minus a skull; and into the strange story of what happened that skull and how it came from Lough Key to Lough Erne. Music and myth and merriment and poetry go all through this book, deftly changing places like expert step-dancers. There is the wisdom, too, of old age, ancestral wisdom, and the innocence of youth and first love, and the learning that a young man picks up from lake and woodland, from rocky hill and from the creatures that inhabit wild places.

A night spent listening to Paddy Tunney is only to be matched by a day with him abroad in Ireland: once I went with him from Galway to Carn and from Carn to Dublin by way of Con Corrigan's in Clogher; I've listened to him sing the night through in a house in Clontarf, all the night through on cups of tea, singing from the heart and never once repeating himself.

At the centre of all that music on Lough Erne shore was the mother, singing as delicately as her hands embroidered, judging carefully what songs she should pass on, when and why. He comes to her one long bright evening, as he says: "coming into the mouth of the mowing". Pat Gormley has stirred his curiosity by telling him that if anyone can sing a certain song it will be Paddy's own mother, so shrewdly he picks his evening and season and makes his request. Remembering, he paints for us a lovely picture: "Meadow mane rippled with corncrakes and scythe steel sang to whetstone. The air ached with the pain and joy of living. It was the time that turned my mother to songs of love and longing, and the two lines from *The false bride* I had asked her about, a fortnight before, gently jerked her mind towards them.

"She put aside the hoops that held the cloth, where her needle and thread has wrought the most exotic rosebuds, open flowers and intricate patterns, and wove with her voice arabesques of sound that bested the embroidery. She sang me for the first time that exquisitely beautiful song: *As I roved out* or *The false bride.*"

From a faraway Fermanagh evening, preserved here forever by this Man of Song, the scene comes to us and the poignant words:

> Now at night when I go to my bed of slumber
> The thoughts of my truelove run on my mind
> When I turn around to embrace my darling
> Instead of gold sure it's brass I find
> And I wish the queen would call home her armies
> From the West Indies, America and Spain
> And every man to his wedded woman
> In hopes that you and I would meet again.

If you were to ask me which song I prefer of all that I've heard Paddy Tunney sing, I'd swither between, say, *The mountain streams* and *Moorlough Mary* and *The buachaill roe,* settling for the three of them and in that order of preference. If you were to ask me which of his stories I prefer I'd be hard put to it to make a choice. They are here in God's profusion and I envy the reader who comes to them for the first time: stories of people and loved places, memories of his youth, legends of the past, the whole imaginative life of a loughshore that is one of the most interesting corners of Ireland.

Forty or so years ago I first encountered Paddy Tunney in the office of a Dublin newspaper, and listened to him talk about everything from prison to poetry, and about my brother and about Séamus de Faoite, both of whom had already told me a lot about him. It was the beginning of a friendship that I have found a most rewarding joy. This book crystallises much of what those forty years have brought me. To any reader approaching it I confidently wish the same joy in the journey.

Benedict Kiely

The lark in the morning she rises off her nest
And goes up in the air with the dew on her breast
Like a jolly ploughboy she whistles and she sings
And comes home in the evening with the dew on her wings

The singer was a pleasant man with a clear complexion and a fine, flowing beard. As he dandled me on his knee and repeated the verse I found myself joining him in the song. I was a man of four summers then and very fond of my song-master. But when he ceased singing and told me tales of Stoics and Spartans I was transported to another world beyond time and far from the moorlands of Minchyfinn and Meenatully with their purple heather and blazing whin.

Came a day in the autumn of that year and I was brought into a room where my songmaster lay in a deep sleep, a peaceful smile lighting up his countenance. Roddy Sheils knelt by the bedside and he was crying. I had never seen a big man cry before and it was a frightening experience.

Only then I noticed the two lighted candles and the crucifix by the bedside. Well, I'd be a Stoic and would not cry. So I knelt down and said my prayers like the rest. He was now safe from demons and heathens and the cat-breacs he had told me so much about.

In spite of the Stoicism I practised with great difficulty and much lip-biting, it was decided that I should go to my Granny's in Mollybreen that evening. I would get a well buttered ceapair of bread with sugar on top, I was told, and Aunt Brigid would teach me to play the melodeon.

So I took my last fond leave of my songmaster, who was also my maternal grandfather, and set out with the enthusiasm of a Livingstone to explore the mystery and magic of distant Mollybreen. It mattered little that it

was only a townland away. To me it was the well at the
world's end.

On the way I had to pass Roddy's Pocket, that tiny plot
of a field where Roddy Sheils declared he grew potatoes so
large that he could sit on one end of a tuber and take his
dinner off the other end. Then there was the Ranny that
jutted far out into the lough, where hares held council and
wild ducks disported themselves. At the narrows where the
boat was moored, Roddy had sworn to me that he had often
seen trout rise so high for a sedge or a daddy-long-legs that
they cope-carlied in the air and came on to dry land. Only
with great wriggling and springing on their tails did they
succeed in reaching water again. "If you had been there at
the time", he assured me, "with a wee grain of salt to shake
on their tails you'd have no bother catching a bagful of them."

West of the Ranny were the Black Banks and Scairt Island
where the presence of long-legged wading birds heralded a
break in fine weather. Thereabouts, black, glossy-coated
otters were wont to appear at dusk and vanish under bur-
rowed banks at the approach of man.

Far and away the most exciting visitor to Mollybreen was
the *waterhorse,* a prancing white stallion that came ashore at
full moon or when mares were in season. Most of his time
was spent at the bottom of the lough in a Tírnanóg for steeds,
where, it would seem, mares were a scarce commodity and in
great demand. Contact with the waterhorse invariably meant
the loss of a mountainy mare, for he put the comehither on
almost every equine female he encountered and led her away
to his kingdom under the water. Only once did his elopement
plan fail and it happened this way:

Mick Fada, who lived in Tamur, (*Chower*) kept a tidy little
mare. He bought her when she was a foal, made an incision in
her tail and inserted a clove of garlic to guard her against
natural diseases and the potent spell of the waterhorse. Mick
generally brough her to be served by Uncle Johnny's stallion
in Mollybreen when she was in heat, and so, in the latter end,
she headed away for Mollybreen herself when she felt romantic.

This evening in late spring didn't the dithering come on Mick's mare and she duly arrived in Mollybreen at milking time. Johnny and the stallion were away in Shannagh, putting out dung on a cut of lea for the cousins, and would not be back for a couple of days. Uncle Dan turned the mare out on the rough ground beyond the wee byre and went on with his work. He forgot that the moon was full or he'd have secured her in the stable.

Next morning he found her stretched out for dead at the foot of the meadow near the lough. The ground about her was trampled and pounded as if with hooves, and a couple of mouthfuls of hair were missing from her mane. He was very annoyed and sent for her owner.

"It waishe the waterhorshe," Mick lamented, "but she beshted him. Look how he waishe trying to trail her away into the lough. Poor Fanny," — that was her name — "she died for virtue!"

Poor Mick, it was little he knew of the moral fibre of mares! "It would be a pity to bury her skin and all", ruminated Mick. "Damn it, Dan, we'll skin her", and he drew a big barber knife out of his pocket and began operations. Dan fetched the shoemaker's knife out of a drawer in the kitchen dresser and gave him a hand. When they had completed their task, Dan went off for spades and a shovel to dig a grave. With that, the mare gave a snort, struggled to her feet and away she goes galloping and neighing round the meadow like the hammers of hell. Mick Fada nearly fell out of his standing.

The mare was not dead but she had fainted with the exertions of an all night love-making session with the water-horse! Great bother the two men had in catching the skinless beast and grafting the skin back again on her with the aid of black sally scollops. But Mick could never put harness on that mare again. You see the scollops grew and Mick was afraid to pull them out in case the animal would bleed to death. So he kept her till she died and cut the scollops that grew profusely on her back every year and sold them at the market in Ballyshanny. She had bested the waterhorse sure enough, but she had no inclination to go a-mating again.

I never met the waterhorse or any of the ghosts during my stay in Mollybreen, but I noticed that my Granny shook the Holy Water to the four corners of the house at Rosary time each night.

Aunt Brigid played the melodeon and played it with a will. The mockery and magic of the music she coaxed from that old box brought the great reel dancers of the mountain to many a floor, where the crigs of hobnails on the flagstones sent splanks flying to the rafters.

I failed to master the melodeon or indeed to shape the simplest of tunes on it. The *Keelero,* one of the easiest tunes to play, was a Connachtman I never managed to wrestle. However, I picked up many old reels and set dances from my aunt and these I lilted to myself when out sailing goose-feather boats on the big waterhole between the carthouse and the Black Park.

But Aunt Brigid was not a singer. Neither was Uncle Johnny, in spite of the gulder that issued from his lips when commanding his sheepdogs. The only song I ever heard him attempt was *MacAdoo.* He inclined to the declamatory style and the tone could scarcely be described as melodious.

My other paternal uncle, whose name was Dan, didn't sing either but he whistled a tune merrily and was a fastidious, if limited, performer on the melodeon. Moreover, he danced a reel with restraint but with great exactitude.

Johnny, on the other hand, performed with the abandon of a Salome but without her saving grace or consummate skill. His role was that of jester at the kitchen dances of the mountain and indeed he was the scourge of the sophisticated and polished reel dancers.

Francey Monaghan, Denis McMeniman, Pat's Francey and George Walsh would arrive outside the house, where the dance was to be held, in wader boots or hobnails. Wrapped up carefully in a brown paper parcel were the black dancing shoes, so well polished that you could almost see yourself in them. The waders or hobnails were removed and stashed away in a creel in the carthouse or hidden in a clump of rushes near the house. The heavy, hand-knit socks were discarded and the feet that had been well washed with the potato water of that day's boiling, to remove even the suspicion of an ache, were inspected by match light. Dainty, fine shop hose, with elegant patterns of squares and diamonds imprinted upon them, were slid smoothly over toes, heels and ankles, and then the feet were insinuated into the magic "shoon". Careful lacing and tying completed the operation. She would be a dull and insensitive damsel indeed who failed to admire such footwear under trousers with a crease that would cut your throat.

And the secret of that cut-throat crease that only mountain reel dancers aspired to, and that had baffled journeyman improvers, William the Tailor and other renowned wielders of the tailor's goose? Well, the dancing dervish smoothed and ironed his trousers with an ordinary smoothing iron. Then the precious article of clothing was placed between two sheets of heavy, brown paper under the bedtick and he lay on them for seven nights. Such dedication went not unrewarded.

Uncle Johnny's preparation for the dance was, in contrast, slipshod in the extreme. No fault could be found with his mode of shaving, it is true. He used the old, open, cut-throat razor and no man from Mizzen Head to Malin could best him in honing a scythe, a reaping-hook or a razor. He was not content to mow a meadow. He skinned it, and, when it came to shaving, even a bristle root was in peril.

But his footwork preparation was faulty. The boots were hobnailed and encassed feet that were given to corns and were on the large side even for a big man. It seemed that their manipulation on a flagstone floor was a feat far beyond the ability of their master. Indeed a tiny wisp of a man who feared Johnny and was always making jokes about him behind his back, once quipped somewhat uncharitably that such feet were meant only for the purpose of tramping flax in a dam. Johnny came to hear the remark and was not amused. He bided his time for he was too old a cat to be bucked by a kittling. Ten years later, when the little man died in a state of abject penury, and some kindly neighbour inquired quietly: "Do you think who'll supply the coffin?" Johnny bawled back: "Beged! Maguire and Patterson! Who else do you think?"

Behold Johnny on his way to the dance, an ashplant under his oxter, a peaked cap perched high on his head and his navy blue jacket, greening with age, tightly buttoned. He never wore an overcoat. There was no crease in his trousers. They were narrow and kneed and under them the toes of immense pavers turned up towards their wearer.

Johnny could elbow and jundy his way through the Quadrilles and Lancers with the best of them. At a Highland Fling he could pass himself reasonably well, although he did cover a lot of ground. When it came to the two-hand reel, that was the pride and joy of that mountainy region — indeed their unique showpiece to dazzle the people of the plains and the valleys — Johnny's performance was a carricature of the prize dancers and a great embarrassment to them. At the dance Francey Monaghan and George Walsh were first on the floor, to be followed by Feilim Gallagher and Denis McMeniman. Johnny leaped out on the floor, dragging a lesser known reel dancer with him.

For the first few turns all went well, but when Francey Monaghan "snuffed the candle" and Denis McMenimam followed on with the simmie dimmies of the famed screwing step, it was the signal for Johnny to cut loose. With a wild whoop that drowned the melodeon music, he took a buckleap into the air, landed on his heels and the candle, that those two mighty toeplates failed to snuff, would have a flame like a bonfire on Saint John's Eve.

His performance drew great belly laughter from the assembly and completely stole the thunder of the accomplished dancers.

Only with the arrival of the famed Lough Dearg pair, Charlie Colton and Willie Swift McCafferty, and the execution of the feat of low flying and intricate leg-looping that marked their inimitable style of reel dancing, was a sense of proportion and dignified appreciation restored to that gathering. "Fair wind and ripe corn!" some old-timer used to shout and the dancers re-doubled their efforts. Then when Swift performed some well-nigh impossible gyration, someone responded with the cry of: "House come out of the window!"

Many years later, I tried to recapture that kitchen dance scene in a poem I called *Reelsong:*

Bind sultry silence in thongs of thunder, and ropes
    of laughter round the rigging sweel.
Across the flagstones where dancers pivot
    their hobnails rivet a rousing reel.
All fiddle-frenzied the feet are flying and legs
    are lacing in a hundred loops.
Now fast they're wheeling to face the music
    and handclaps hail them and lusty whoops.

An old man bred in the mountain marrow stands
    up to harrow where the dancers ploughed
A troubadour from the heights of glory he
    tells his story of love aloud.
The greeshagh glows, the strong mouth quivers,
    from throat there rivers like rain in drouth
A song that leaps down the lanes of longing
    and hones a hunger for the Land of Youth

It was not for his nimble-footed reel dancing, however, that Willie McCafferty bore the honourable name of Swift. It is no descriptive adjective. Willie's father, James McCafferty, was a satiric bard with an incisive style reminiscent of the great Dean himself. The excercise of his witty talent got him into all kinds of tangles with self-righteous neighbours and sanctimonious old hags. They knew little of the great bardic tradition he was perpetuating but dreaded the blistering ranns he composed.

Complaints relative to James Swift McCafferty's literary effusions were not infrequently lodged with the parish priest and that august dignitary, as others of the cloth had attempted to do with Owen Rua and Cathal Buí before him, set out to silence the songster. But James Swift was as elusive as the Scarlet Pimpernell and it was only after many forays into the wilds around Lough Dearg shore that he at last ran him to ground. The jarvey, on the instructions of the priest, pulled the sidecar across the narrow road so that Swift's last escape

route was blocked. He stood his ground and faced the wrath
of the fiery Father Ryan.

"James McCafferty", began the priest in stern and severe
tones, "why do you torture and distress your neighbours, and
my parishioners, with your vile and scurrilous rhymes?" Not
for one moment did James Swift lose his composure. He
removed his cap reverently and begged forgiveness:

> O Father Ryan, you, most divine,
> Your mercy I implore!
> Pardon me for this one crime,
> And I'll transgress no more.

The sudden poetic sally was too much for the priest. "Drive
on, Johnny, drive on", he commanded his jarvey, "or he'll
make a song on myself."

There was much poteen-making in those parts around that
time. Hugh Gallagher lived in Rusheen on the other side of
the road from my grandfather's home. I can clearly recall the
day he lured me into his kitchen to see the complete "tacklings". There was a still on the huge turf fire, a still-head sealed
to the still with special sealing glue (home-made and
known as "Luding"), a wonderful copper pipe with many
bends, known as a worm, and a huge wooden barrel filled
with water. Into the still was put the potel or barrem or wash,
whichever you wished to call the fermented malt and sugar.
When the contents came to the boil the steam was driven
through the still-head into the worm housed in the barrel.
There the cooling effect of the water caused the steam to
condense and trickle from the protruding end of the worm
into a trapping vessel. The liquor so distilled was known as
singlings and had to be distilled a second time before it was
poteen-whiskey.

The whole operation filled me with awe and fear. When
the first poteen finally came through, Hugh ceaped it in a
small vessel and threw the contents over the half door. "Away
and watch for us!" he commanded some invisible ally. He
then came back and drew off the rest of the "heating". "Why
did you do that?" I asked him. "Man dear", he told me, "you
must treat the fairies. If you didn't you'd get no poteen at all,

only water." Experts have told me since that there is a far
sounder reason for discarding the first liquor that comes
through. They maintain that it is unadulterated poison and
would kill even a poteen maker.

He invited me back the next day but my mother would
not let me go. So Hugh, or Coote, as myself and my two sisters called him, came to visit us instead. He said he'd be my
new songmaster and promptly began to teach myself and my
two sisters a song he called *Tagglieownie:*

Her mother had a nice wee dog,
    she used to call it Tony,
And every time I kissed the girl
    he bit my Tagglieownie.

My mother said it wasn't a nice song and rebuked poor old
Coote for teaching children such words. So we learned no
more couplets of the *Tagglieownie,* but he was adamant that
the air would be taught to us. And so it went, in Coote's
curious lilting language:

O audie, audie, audie, audie, audie, audie, audie.
O audie, audie, audie, audie, audie, audie, audie.

Perhaps the only serious rival to Coote's one-word song is
that rousing Kerry composition, *Farranfore.*

Across the moor where, all summer, boglarks corkscrewed
song into the high dome of heaven, lived George McGee, or
George of the whinbush, as he was called. It was a fitting
title for his home, for it was buried in a blaze of whin blossom from early spring until autumn. There was no day he
didn't pay us at least one visit and we re-christened him Peggie,
for whatever reason I do not know.

George, too, made an effort to sing but he had only one
song. It went like this:

That the stones of the street may turn up the pig's feet
If ever I cease to the love.
That the tay may come down to three ha'pence a pound
If ever I cease to the love.

My mother said that it wasn't a very good song but there was
no harm in singing it. She promised that, when my grandfather was dead twelve months and her period of mourning
over, she would teach me many songs. It was a promise she
kept.

A year passed and our family moved to Mulleek *(Mew-lick)* in the county of Fermanagh near the banks of Lower Lough Erne. This was a land where men walked and talked tall and there was a rich music in their mode of speech. It was about the time of the building of the Boa Island bridges and roadway and every able-bodied man in the district was employed bridge-building or road-making there. My father got a job on the bridges. All the middle-aged men learned to ride bicycles and bought heavy, surplus army machines to propel themselves to and from work.

Some of the older men learned to master the "iron horse" by sheer perseverance and total concentration. For instance, most of them could not raise their heads to bid you the time of day without falling off their bikes or diving headlong into the roadside shough. The majority of them never managed to dismount with dignity but instead fell off, hoping that none of the neighbours noticed them.

There was a Welsh family whose father came over to manage the felspar mines in Upper Scardan during the Great War. His name was Roberts and when the war ended the mines closed down. However, the Welshman was given a key post on the Boa Island project. Most of the workers were recruited through him and were under the impression that they were beholden to him for their jobs. Mr Roberts made them no wiser and indeed he was charmed when all species of domestic fowl were given to him as gifts. These included ducks, drakes, geese, ganders, cock chickens and great strutting turkey-cocks. His outhouse became one mighty clucking, cackling, quacking, wheezing, gobbling flurry of feathers. So congested did it become, that Mr Roberts was forced to exercise the species with the low-slung chassis in a boghole beside his bungalow.

Indeed Hughie's John once told me that the sky over his house was often blacked out by a flight of birds homing their way back to Tullaghawaine (*Toll-a-wan-ya*), Derryrona and Derrintrig from the hungry alts of Upper Scardan. He couldn't eat them all at once and the problem of feeding them became acute.

So, by degrees, Roberts let it be known that himself and his good wife would prefer to be invited to little banquets in various houses throughout the country where they could devour the birds without the bother of killing, plucking and cooking them. He also intimated that it would greatly add to their enjoyment if a bottle of good Irish whiskey was available to wash down the food.

My father, like the others, fell a victim to this ploy, not through any fault of Roberts, but by way of suggestion from Aunt Minnie, who was staying with us at the time. She held that it was the custom to entertain these people and, as such, would have to be observed. My mother did not see eye to eye with her in this matter. She did not mind providing the food but the very mention of whiskey coming into the house made her very angry indeed. She hated the stuff to the day she died. However, Minnie had her way. So Mr. Roberts and his wife, together with a daughter Annie, who drove a pony and trap and courted B-men, and their two wild sons, Gwyllem and Abraham, descended upon us like a plague of locusts one Sunday evening.

Mr. Roberts was a friendly man and wore a well-cut, charcoalgrey suit with a waistcoat and a gold watchchain hanging across his breast, with a glittering penant attached. His wife was dark and expansive of bosom, with a rich, contralto singing voice. Aunt Minnie whispered awesomely that she spoke Welsh fluently and sang in that language only. She also consumed rather large measures of Irish whiskey, which was an accomplishment uncommon among females at that time.

The wild sons ate all before them and, when asked to sing, refused and were rude to their parents. Annie, the daughter, had good manners and was most correct in her behaviour.

When she imbibed the smallest thimbleful of the fiery liquor,
she gazed wistfully into the fire, no doubt, we children
thought, conjuring up thoughts of her B-man lover with his
putty leggings and clumsy rifle. The thoughts of youth were
indeed long, long thoughts.

There were other guests too. Paddy McMahon, the fiddler,
was among them, for he was wooing Aunt Minnie with all his
might and main at the time. Paddy was from the heathery
country where they always had a good supply of black turf
and were famous for their big hearty hearth fires. His father
was first to be buried in the new graveyard at the back of
Muleek chapel. After the funeral Paddy duly lamented his
father as was the custom with the bardic school. "It's a black
day for the McMahons", he murmured, "when my father was
buried in cold Tierygannon, where the only fuel or fire they
ever had was their neighbour's hazel bush!" A fine dirge indeed, couched in the heroic tradition, but a trifle uncharit-
able towards the men of Tierygannon.

There were other guests too of course; boys and girls from
the neighbourhood, expert set dancers, spoiling for sport and
fun. Still, the Roberts held the limelight and most of the local
boys gave Annie a good show. Indeed it was Roberts who
inspired one of the classic sayings in the Mulleek idiom:
"Roberts gups", he says. "He gwins in that gap." ran the saying. It translates: "Roberts goes up. He goes in in that gap."
The "gups" and "gwins" are merely a welding together of
contractions. "He says", when used with the subtle cunning
of country speech, lends a flavour to the words far beyond
the call of grammar or syntax.

It was a time of great talk about borders and boundary commissions and the Free State and the Six Counties. James Craig was mentioned a good deal and it was said he hated Catholics. Still he permitted the teaching of Irish in the Six County schools so he might not be as bad as he was painted.

When I went to Derryhallow Public Elementary School in 1927, at the ripe old age of six years, I first heard the word Protestant pronounced "Prodesun". There was a family of these creatures attending a school of that persuasion some three miles away and we sometimes met them on the road. The bigger boys told me to shun them like a plague, until I was big enough to beat the lard out of them.

"Yellow belly, green guts, eat the frogs on Friday", was the rhyme a wild boy taught me to shout at them. I learned it off by heart and longed to shout it at them, but my mother forbade me to do so.

Then my neighbours, the O'Connors, heard I could sing and bribed me, with one B.B. toffee each day for a week, to learn the eviction song about Father McFadden and sub-inspector Martin that "gave it tight" to Protestants and tyrants. I quickly picked up the song from my mother but declined to tell her for what purpose, and duly sang it in the field where I was herding as the O'Connors passed on the road with their two Protestant friends and a greyhound they called Daisy.

"Wheesht to you hear that lovely song", Patrick commanded and the four boys stood as still as four statues.

Come all you Roman Catholics and listen to my song
I hope you'll pay attention, I won't detain you long
Concerning Father McFadden who lies in Derry jail
He has been returned for trial since the jury won't take bail

It was on a Sunday Morning just after he said Mass
'Twas the Sub-Inspector Martin was the man did him arrest
He tore the collar off his coat, he had a broad-sword in his hand
He said: "You are my prisoner and with me come along!"

When the people saw their priest a prisoner at their door
David being amongst them, a stone he did procure
He placed the stone all in a sling, and by the Lord's command
He killed the sub-inspector on the ground where he did stand

They put him on a covered coach, Lord Leitrim by his side
And going along the country road he got a speedy ride
The people laughed and jeered at him, 'twas a joyful tale to tell
To see the sub-inspector going away on a door to hell

The Devil met him at the gates and sang a merry song
Saying: "You're welcome Mister Martin, I've waited for you long
The heat will not agree with you, your head will be too sore
And you'll curse the day you strayed away to the mountains of
     Gweedore."

The song over, one of the Protestant boys raised himself
on the stone fence, called a ditch in those parts, and hissed
"Fenian bastard" whereupon the two O'Connors fell on their
Protestant friends and trounced them sevendably.

My mother was much put out by the whole performance.
She told me what a Fenian was but the second word was so
evil, she warned me, that anyone uttering it was in grave
danger of being struck straight down to hell. When I'd grow
older she'd explain it's meaning, she promised, but she
assured me I wasn't one anyhow.

About this time the picture of the United Irishmen, that
my mother displayed proudly in Rusheen, found it's way to
our house in Mulleek. My mother cleaned it and rehung it
over the fireplace. I pestered her with questions about the
men of '98 and Father Murphy. So she sat down and wrote
to Aunt Minnie in Glasgow for the words of the song *Boolavogue*. With great difficulty I learned the words of the song,
for my mother had to read them to me. All her other songs
she had off by heart and so it was much easier learning them.

Came a day in July and a head inspector was to visit the

school. For weeks before we had been polishing up Kipling's
If and *The Burial Of Sir John Moore* and such imperial hog-
wash, to make a favourable impression on the man of learning. The Principal, who was a Monaghan woman, met him at
the door and solicited from him the staggering piece of information that his name was Mister Doak.

In spite of his name, he seemed to be an affable fellow and
quickly took us through geography which, at that time, was
limited to Great Britain and the British Dominions, on which,
they never tired of telling us, the sun never set. He then tested
us with some problems in arithmetic, algebra and euclid.

Then we were released for a short time to ventilate our
brains in the bogs of Derryhallow, while Mister Doak partook
of refreshments with the teachers. The afternoon was devoted
to English with all its works and pomps. Grammar and
composition presented no problems. Indeed he complimented
some of us on our use of that language. The reading seemed
to please him and then he asked for volunteer reciters. A
biggish boy, who afterwards joined the police, stood up and,
with a nasal intonation that would put to rout even the most
foghornish Connemara sean-nós singer, buried Sir John Moore
darkly at the dead of night, wrapping him up in great lea sods
that he coped with his bayonet. He was followed by Johnny
Gallagher, who gave a most grizzly and original rendition of
that wonderful poem, *Whooh!* You known the one:

> Away in the forest all darksome and deep
> The wolves went a-hunting while men were asleep,

to the consternation of the teachers and the delight of Mister
Doak.

"And what of the girls?" the Principal made bold to ask,
throwing in her shock troops to redeem the situation. Up
sprang Jennie Bates, who embarrassed us boys with her lisp-
ing accent and outsized breasts and declaimed Kipling's *If* in
a manner that would have warmed the cockles of Queen Vic-
toria's heart. The clouds dispersed and the sun shone again.
Jennie Bates was followed by Rose Monaghan, who gave
Tennyson's *Brook* such a race to the brimming river that she

reached the winning post well ahead of the stream that, after all, waited to wind about and in and out.

Last but not least we had Murphins Early, who never was late, in Mark Anthony's speech from Julius Ceasar: "Friends, Romans, countrymen . . ."

"Very good", said Mister Doak, "and now we shall have some singing." The teachers were taken completely by surprise. They hadn't reckoned he'd test our singing prowess. By degrees we were gentled through *Merry Little Gipsies Are We, O The Boating Lightly Floating Merrily Away* and *Do You Ken John Peel* and such harmless inanities. It would appear that traditional singing survived in spite of the schools and not because of them. Then the head inspector pulled his last stroke. Was there a boy or a girl who would, or could, sing a song of the people, he inquired, one he or she had learned outside of school. I waited in vain and then, since the wise had not spoken . . .

The song was *Boolavogue,* sung with all the fire and feeling I could muster. The teachers were petrified. Mister Doak shut his eyes and permitted the suggestion of a smile to play across his countenance. When the song was over he thanked me and gave me half-a-crown. "Tis a pity, " he said to the teachers, "a great pity. You know we should be teaching history in the schools." I never met him again.

Barney Deery who lived in the house above us was not a great singer. Once when I had earned the ceapair by helping him to drive a cow to the bachelor, he struck up a stave as I sat munching the long slice of soda bread thickly buttered and iced over with brown sugar.

> O I met with Napper Tandy and he took me by the hand
> Saying how is dear old Ireland and how does she stand
> She's the most distressful country that ever you have seen
> For they're hanging men and women for the wearing of the Green
> So shoulder high your hurleys boys, and grasp your rifles tight
> The mangy bulldog let him bark; he's got no teeth to bite
> When English law can paint the moon and put the Hun to flight
> Then we'll shed our rebel coats and put the hurleys out of sight

"I learned that verse in America", he told me, the fire flashing from his eyes. I made haste to inquire if he had any other songs. "Well, no; that's the only snatch of a song I could ever say I knew", he replied with a finality that would put to flight the most formidable interrogator. "My interest was in philosophy, the Harry Shuttle and black magic." He was referring to Aristotle of course. "Young fellow did you ever hear of the Elixir of Life or the Philosopher's Stone?"

I replied that I had not and could not disguise the wonder and amazement that gripped me to learn that Barney had such an interest in the like. Barney warmed to his subject. "Well you see", he went on, "old Master Kane was a very clever man. He taught us bits of Greek and Latin in the old hedge-school he ran at night for grown-up men. He broke us in on philosophy with the book of the Harry Shuttle as well. We were just starting on black magic when I went away to America.

"I was away more years than I'd care to admit but when I

came home again hadn't I a hive of very troublesome neighbours to contend with. They'll tell you that bad fences make
bad neighbours, but it's my considered opinion that the hen
that lays in the neighbour's nettles has caused more wars and
rumours of wars than Helen of Troy herself.

"Faldie McGware, who lived down there in that house you
are living in now, was as twisted and contrary as the hindlegs
of a dog. But, if he was itself, he couldn't hold the candle to
his sons. There were two of them in it and they were the
divils out of hell. We differed about hens that laid out and
war broke out. Not a day passed that we hadn't at least one
battle. They were good stone throwers and I wasn't bad at
the same either. They were in the hollow and I was on the
height so Barney had the whip hand.

"Then they made slings and the war began to go against
me. They didn't leave me a sound pane in the windows and
the roof was so paved with stones that when Johnny Denis
came to thatch after they moved out he wore the knees out
of three pairs of leather breeches.

"I was at my wit's end to get even with them so, when
young Master Kane read out of *Old Moore's Almanac* one
night I was making my ceili with him, that Professor Hairycat
of Bristol University had at last discovered the Philosopher's
Stone and was willing to mail on a fragment of it to interested
parties for as little as five pounds, I decided to play my ace.

"I got the Master to write away for a chunk of the stone
and we enclosed a fiver. You see the Old Master had taught
us that not only did the stone turn baser metals into gold but
that it would also turn baser mortals into pillars of salt. It
would be a rare old revenge to have the three McGwares
rooted to the ground as three pillars of salt that the cows
would be licking in dry weather. Then with the first hurricane of rain they'd be washed off the face of the earth altogether.

"In the fullness of time the stone arrived by registered post
and tied up with as many straps and strillions as a mummer's
hat but no matter how I turned it I couldn't turn the McGwares
into the pillars of salt. Then, one night, they left and went

away to live in the Free State. Master Kane declared that that was even a worse fate than befell Lot's wife."

Poor Barney, he had been to America right enough but it was whispered he had got sunstroke. This left him "not quite the full shilling", it was feared. When my father found him a fortnight after, half-drowned in a shough of water into which he had fallen with a heavy burden of hay on his back, his first exclamation was: "Ah! Paddy, it was Faldie done this on me!"

Mrs. Kelly and Thomas, who bought Barney's land and renovated the house, came all the way from far off Philadelphia. They brought with them a gramophone and a fine selection of records. For us it was a nine days' wonder and the first machine of its kind to make an appearance in our midst. There were records of John McCormack, the Flanagan Brothers and many other Irish-American performers. The Kellys were neither singers nor musicians but acted as the catylist to release the great surge of song and music inherent in our heritage. To them we must be eternally grateful.

Fast on the heels of the Kellys came Australian Joe. His full name was Joe (Fada) Gallagher and he was a first cousin of my mother and the son of Mary Gallagher of The Mountain Streams. He had emigrated to Australia after the Great War and had struck it rich. A handsome, flamboyant romantic, who had made his dream come true, he was a great favourite with the fair sex. He even succeeded in dating the Principal of our school, a formidable task. Now a sugar cane grower in North Queensland, he could well afford the chauffeur-driven car that carried him on his peregrinations round this little Isle of Green from Killarney to the Giant's Causeway. He had bought a gramophone in London and forwarded it to our address along Lough Erne shore. This avoided delays in delivery. My mother was understandably slow in accepting the huge parcel, for she was unaware of its contents or true destination, but scarcely had the puzzled and curious postman taken his departure, when Joe's unheralded arrival resolved her problem.

She was seated near the kitchen window sprigging away

when he peered in over the half-door. In a flash they were hugging and embracing and tears of joy and sorrow chased each other down their cheeks. It was then I heard for the first time that mighty song, *The Mountain Streams where the Moorcocks Crow*. Although my mother always maintained that she couldn't "put the silk on it" like her Aunt Mary, I am convinced she was being unduly humble. Here's the great song as she used to sing it:

I said: "My darling, if you'll wed a rover
My former raking I will leave aside
Here is my hand and I pledge my honour
If you prove constant I'll make you my bride."

"If my parents knew that I loved a rover
Great affliction I would undergo.
I'll stop at home for another season near
The Mountain Streams Where The Moorcocks Crow."

"If my parents knew that I loved a rover
They would tie me down with strong iron bands
And in a dungeon they would confine me
Where is no comfort of any kind.
Now I'll away and acquaint my parents.
I hope my absence will not cause a blow.
I'm happy here though I may be courted from
The Mountain Streams Where The Moorcocks Crow."

"Then farewell darling for another season.
I hope we'll meet in yon woodland vale.
And when we meet we'll embrace each other.
I'll pay attention to your love-sick tale.
It's hand in hand we will join together and
I'll escort you to yon valley low
Where the linnet sings her sweet notes so pleasing near
The Mountain Streams Where The Moorcocks Crow."

Joe's gramophone was carried over moorland and mountain and across the border by an unapproved route until it reached his father's home in Tamur in the county Donegal. Joe bought up every available record on the market at the time. Indeed it was the endless sessions of song, dance, story-telling and music, stimulated by his home-coming, that brought together again a people whose pride and self-reliance had been blighted by the bitterness of the Civil War.

For me his supreme act was in persuading my mother to sing *The Mountain Streams,* for although she frequently extolled the merits of her Aunt Mary's singing of it, she had never before sung it for me. Twenty years later when I had grown to manhood and weathered many a gale, I prevailed on her to teach me the song.

The 'thirties brought hunger and hardships to many a hearth along the loughside. The potato crop was poor and there was no sun to save the turf. The old people were predicting that it would be another "winter of the bad fires". So it came to pass that when a neighbour who was in making his ceili suggested to my father that there was fire-wood enough on his lands in Rossmore to keep both our chimneys reeking, he joined forces with the neighbour's sons, and together all three of them hewed and carted home supplies of ash and beech to substitute for the turf. On Saturdays I went with them and hacked away with a small hand-hatchet.

I can clearly recall a Saturday in winter when the Mule Park Bay had frozen over. When we had eaten the meagre lunch we had brought with us, we ventured out on the ice to test its strength. After skating for a short while we returned and had just begun to saw and hatchet again, when a cart from the shooting lodge up the road trundled by, bearing trunks, cases and such trappings.

Behind it walked three, tall, lean, well-dressed men who had just arrived by train for the shooting. The had come from England and some of the locals held them in awe, though for what reason I never could find out.

"Stop!" shouted one of the neighbours. His brother and my father stopped work and stood awkwardly to attention. I purposely ignored the command, hacked away and sang a rousing stave. When the strangers passed on I was harshly rebuked for showing disrespect to the "gentlemen". "Gentlemen", I blurted out disdainfully, "I read somewhere that one of them is a gaffer in a coal-mine and that another owns a tannery!" It was the only time I felt compelled to answer my father back. Even at the age of nine, I was furious that the

whip-lash of oppression had cut so deeply into the pride of
the people. Emancipation my foot!

Nineteen thirty-two was a year of hope and promise. "We
never died a winter yet and the devil wouldn't kill us in
summer", the old people used to say. There was to be a
general election in the Free State and chances were that De
Valera would come to power. Dublin was to host the Eucha-
ristic Congress:

O My Dark Rosaleen, do not sigh do not weep,
The priests are on the ocean green they march along the deep
There's wine from the royal Pope, upon the ocean green
And Spanish ale will bring you hope, my Dark Rosaleen.

A newspaper was started in Dublin called *The Irish Press*
and Roddy The Rover wrote a feature in it every week. He ran
competitions with prizes as high as half-acrown for poems
and rhymes and pieces of local history from school-children
who felt they had a flair for writing.

Big Pat O'Connor bought *The Irish Press* daily and, when
he had read it, passed it on to me. He encouraged me to write
for Roddy The Rover and it was a proud day for both of us
when I won my first half-a-crown.

On a Saturday night at ten o'clock the good news of Dev's
victory reached us by courier from Pettigo. We were gathered
together in O'Connors' in an atmosphere of great expectancy.
Big Pat had told us of his battle with the landlord's agent to
secure possession of his holding and thereby earn the right to
a vote. There was heady talk of the Land League days and
the great hostings held to wring the right of ownership from
the rapacious rackrenters. It was a night of inspired story-
telling and high hope for the future.

Big John Lawn, a local warrior who had beaten up six
members of the old RIC on his own, was there declaiming
the *Sean-Bhean Bhocht* in a voice that made up in zeal what it
lacked in melody:

And will Ireland then be free? says the Sean-Bhean Bhocht
Will Ireland be free? says the Sean-Bhean Bhocht.
Yes, old Ireland will be free, from the centre to the sea.
Then hurrah! for liberty says the Sean-Bhean Bhocht.

When he finished, someone sitting well back in the shadows
started to the tune of *The Pride of Petravore:*

When we were little children Johnny Redmond was a fool
He told us to be satisfied with something like Home Rule
But we have learned a thing or two since we attended school
And we want a republic now in Ireland.

If we had got the proper thing a president would own
The empire with the army and the navy would go down
I know the man who suits us for he fought in Dublin town
The invincible and gallant De Valera.

Chorus
Up De Valera, you're the champion of the fight
We'll follow you to battle 'neath the orange, green and white
When next we tackle England, we will wash her out of sight
And make De Valera president of Ireland.

At Ringsend in Boland's De Valera took his stand
A hundred of the boys at most were there in his command
I'm sure the British tommies they were slightly out of hand
But you couldn't put the blame on De Valera.

And then when the tommies threw their bombs in British style
Their lovely aim made De Valera's men begin to smile
When this took such effect upon the common rank-in-file
Just imagine then the grin on De Valera.

A great day for Ireland will be the winning day.
The boys from every county will be there in grand array
From Donegal to Kerry and from Clare to Dublin Bay
We'll bring out the fighting men of Ireland

There'll be gunmen, pikemen, pipers by the score
We'll carry arms openly as in the days of yore
The defence of the realm won't be heard of anymore
When De Valera's president of Ireland.

The good news had to be spread and what better way to
spread it than by the wildfire beacons that had proclaimed
the glad tidings down the arches of the centuries. Patrick
O'Connor and myself were dispatched to Tonaghgorm island
where the tinder-dry whins took readily to the spark applied
to them and crackled and blazed the joyful tidings out across
the broad bosom of Lough Erne.

We were on our way back when challenged by an RUC constable. I ignored the command to halt but Patrick stood firm and engaged the peeler in verbal combat. After a short, sharp exchange both men withdrew and no blows were struck nor blood spilt. That poor policeman was killed in 1935 during the pogroms in Belfast.

But next morning when we woke, Ireland was not free and things were much the same. Tariff walls were thrown up round the twenty-six counties and the gospel of self-sufficiency was preached and practised with considerable success. The Economic War commenced, for Dev refused to pay the Land Annuities. By degrees he abolished the oath of allegiance to Britain, annulled the treaty, encouraged the farmers to grow wheat and initiated a free beef scheme for the poor people of the country, when no market could be found for the surplus cattle. He was also interested in the promotion of the Irish language.

Smuggling cattle across the border became the chief occupation of every able-bodied man and boy in our parts. Not infrequently I acted as scout for large herds that were being moved over the line under the cover of darkness. Police and customs men were notoriously corrupt and easily bribed. Notwithstanding this, however, the odd Head Constable or District Inspector, who was not in on a particular deal, made a sortie down a border road and seized large herds of lowing kine, for the hirelings invariably ran away.

Men who never owned a four-footed beast in their lives swaggered into fairs, slunging great herds of cattle before them with stout ashplants and slapped hands and exchanged fistfuls of fivers with the biggest cattle dealers in the land. They were only sponsors for the cattle, of course, but when challenged by the police as to ownership of the animals, nonchalantly replied: "They're my own, if I had my debt paid." For each head of cattle they drove into the fair and went through the motions of selling, they collected two pounds from the real owner who had already made the bargain with the purchasers.

It was a fine piece of bluff and one that was only called

when the police went out to the remote hill farms of the
border country and counted the number and colour of the
hairs in the hide of every bovine about the place. It was then
that the border cows began giving birth to twin calves and
triplets in such numbers and with such rapidity that one
Head Constable, who came from the Slieve Gullion area and
was steeped in folklore and mythology, was forced to the
conclusion that the Brown Bull of Cooley had been rein-
carnated and was at his old tricks again. He reminded us all at
a fair in Kesh one fine day that it was recorded in a very old
version of the Táin Bó Cuailgne, or The Cattle Raid of Cooley,
that the famed brown bull could serve seventy heifers in a
session, and that, if by any chance they did not give birth to
twin calves within seven days of the service, they burst asunder
with the force of the begetting. No wonder the Connacht
men were so keen to steel that noble bull of ours!

Seasons came and went. May Eves were full of the bleating of heather-blades and bitterns as they scythed across the swamps and slunks where we busily gathered marsh marigolds to ward off the spells of witches, wizards, speymen or the blinking blight of boyos with the evil eye. Armfuls of the golden blossoms were borne home and spread on thresholds and window-stools or strewn at the barn and byre doors to save and protect ourselves and our cattle from the evil that was abroad on that mysterious night and until first light on May morning.

It is recorded in the Yellow Book of Lecan that, at first light on May Day, Cormac Mac Airt, High King of Ireland, repaired to the ramparts of Tara to make sure that no evil spirits descended upon his kingdom from the upper air. And that is the time the witches of the world "milk the tether". This they do by alighting off their brooms in a meadow field near the centre of a parish and by sweeping the dew of the grass in towards them, chanting all the while: "Come all to me! Come all to me!" In this way they trap the butter of every churning in the parish for the next twelve months. The other women could fill their crocks with yellow cream and thicken it to their hearts' content but, when it comes to the churning, they can jibble away for the run of a day without getting as much butter as would grease the gudgel of a wheelbarrow.

Against these wicked spells the marigolds or mayflowers, or indeed a four-leafed shamrock, are the only plants or herbs known to give complete immunity.

Jamey Houston, a fine fiddle-player from Drumkeen outside of Letterkenny, told me once at a wake, of a siege the witches gave him when he was a wee fellow, one May morning many years ago. It happened like this: Jamey's father had two thieving heifers and the devil himself couldn't keep them out of the neighbour's meadow field. Bad fences make bad neighbours and Jamey's father was not on speaking terms with this neighbour over the head of a mern ditch. So Jamey was roused before dawn every morning and sent out, barefoot, to bring the beasts back as silently as possible.

Just as he jumped the fence into the field didn't he spy this large, four-leafed shamrock growing on the bruagh of the shough, rank and green as a docken on a dunghill. It marked the spot where a young mare had dropped her first foal, he knew, so he plucked it hurriedly and hid it carefully in his breast pocket.

At that moment, the slight streak of grey in the eastern sky was completely blacked out and, looking up, he saw what seemed to be seven great ravens descending on the meadow. In awe, he shinned up a holly bush and concealed himself in the thick leaves. But the objects descending on the dewy grass were not ravens. They were seven black witches astride their brooms! Slowly they alighted and began sweeping the dew towards the centre of the field chanting ominously in unison: "Come all to me! Come all to me!"

To his horror, Jamey recognised four of them and he was frightened out of his wits. Still, curiosity got the better of his fear, and leaning far out to get a better view, he lost his balance and fell headlong down among the hags.

They at once fell to and lambasted him with the balded ends of their broomsticks and then decided to kill him by driving a stake through his heart. Each time they approached with the stake and attempted to drive it home, didn't it boomerang and fell one of the witches instead. The hags were completely bewildered for they did not know he was carrying a four-leafed shamrock. In spite of the protection it afforded him, he could not muster sufficient strength to break through their ranks, so when three of them had been laid low and the others struck their brooms in the ground and approached unarmed, he lay there prostrate, like a rabbit waiting for a weasel to come in and make the kill.

They had resolved to grant him a reprieve, they told him,

on condition that he'd swear, by Crom Cruaidh and his sub-gods twelve, neither to mention the incident nor reveal the identity of the hags he recognised until the last of them had passed through the portals of death. "And I kept my promise!" he added triumphantly.

"But you have just told us the full story now," butted in a a traun fellow from the foothills, who made poteen and twisted the horns of unbranded stray sheep in order to claim them as his own.

"I'm free to speak this blessed night", Jamey gave him back, "the last of the old crones is lying down there in the room a cold corpse!" Even the hard man from the hills was shaken.

And my mother had a beautiful song describing that mysterious hour of dawn, when natural and supernatural powers are said to be most potent. Here it is:

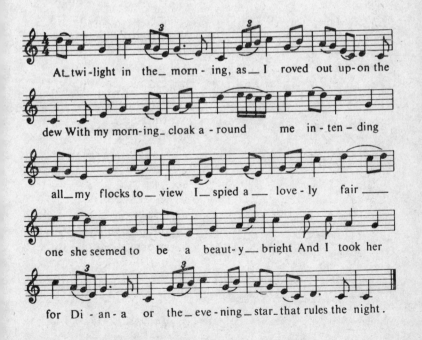

At twi-light in the morn-ing, as I roved out up-on the dew With my morn-ing cloak a-round me in-ten-ding all my flocks to view I spied a love-ly fair one she seemed to be a beaut-y bright And I took her for Di-an-a or the eve-ning star that rules the night.

I being so much surprised by her
it being the forenoon of the day
To see that lovely creature
coming o'er the banks of sweet
Loughrea
Her snow-white breast lay naked
and her cheeks they were a
rosy red
And my heart was caplivated by
the two black eyes rolled in
her head.

Fair maid I cried, your love I crave
for Cupid is a cruel foe
I'll roll you in my morning cloak
and I'll bring you home to
Easter Snow
Go home, aquaint your parents
and indeed kind sir, I'll do
the same
And if both our parents give
consent neither you nor I will
bear the blame.

Her singing of that song dispelled all thoughts of wicked witches or wizards with their black magic and evil.

Mandy Gallagher of Tullagh, Carrigart, in the county of Donegal, had a fine song in praise of the May morning dew that the witches put to such evil purpose for their own gains. Mandy had a great way with a song and, though many of our younger singers attempt to emulate his clarity of tone and sincerity of expression, they sound like very faint echoes of the mighty troubadour himself. Alas! he died young and we hope that "the Eternal Master found that single talent well employed".

And here now is Mandy's *May Morning Dew:*

How plea-sant   in _ win-ter ___ to   sit by__ the hob

List-'ning   to the   barks and the   howls of   a   dog   Or in

sum-mer   to   wan-der__ the wide ___ val-leys through, And to

pluck the__ wild flow-ers__ from the May Morn - ing   Dew.

Summer is coming, oh! summer is here
With the leaves all so green and the sky blue and clear
And the birds they are singing their fond mates to woo
And the flowers they are springing in the May Morning Dew.

God be with the old folk who are now dead and gone
And likewise my brothers, young Denis and John
As we tripped through the heather, the wild hare to pursue
And our joys they were mingled with the May Morning Dew.

The house we were reared in, there's not a stone on a stone
And all round the garden with weeds is o'ergrown
And all the kind neighbours that ever I knew
Like the red rose they are faded from the May Morning Dew.

Indeed it was to that haunting old reel, *New May Day,*
that Denis Feeley, who hailed from the Farrincassidy side
and was hired as a spalpeen in Jimmy Flanagan's, danced his
two-hand reel-hornpipe, faced by the finest female dancer in
the company. On a quiet night with the rambling house door
open, the crigs of his tips and toeplates could be heard down
at Barney Murray's bog.

Not only could my mother sing, she could also turn a tale
with the best storyteller in the land. It was often I heard her
mention the Ceannaí Bán, or the White or Fair Pedlar, who
was boiled alive in a poteen still and buried in a bog bank
because the poteen makers coveted the biorán brollaigh, or
breast-pin, of solid gold that fastened the pedlar's cloak.

The crime was committed near Lough na mBreac Mór,
near Breezy Mountain, and it is said that even to this day, if
you launch an otter-board in that lake in order to capture
one or more of its big trout, it will immediately leap ashore
again, so great is the revulsion of nature for the dark deed
perpetrated thereabouts.

Or again she told us of Supple Corrigan, the famous
Fermanagh raparee, who raced on shank's mare from the out-
skirts of Enniskillen to the banks of the Arney, hotly pursued
by Lord Belmore on one of his fastest chargers. The highway-
man never looked behind him, but with a mighty spring,
cleared the fifty feet span of water before him. Belmore's
anger turned to admiration. "A fine jump, Corrigan, a fine
jump!" he shouted across the stretch of water.

"Devil thank me Belmore", he gave him back, "I had a
long race for it!"

The Loughside was indeed a land of legend. Only a mile
away, at the ruined gatehouse to Castlecaldwell, stands the
famed Stone Fiddle chiselled from limestone quarried near
the spot and erected to the memory of one Denis McCabe,
musician and jester to Sir James Caldwell, Baronet and
Count of Milan. McCabe was a wonderful fiddler but
was given to the drink. It appears that the good knight and
his guests were out on the lake in Saint Patrick's barge, re-
galing themselves with strong liquor and enjoying the music
played by McCabe.

The poor fiddler keeled over and fell into the water. There

was no one on board sober enough to rescue him and so he
drowned. It happened on August 13th 1770, as the inscrip-
tion on the Stone dolefully records and then goes on to deepen
the gloom with the following verse:

Ye fiddlers beware ye fiddlers fate
Don't attempt ye deep lest ye repent too late
Ye ever were to water foes
So shun the deep till it with whiskey flows
On dry land ye can exercise your skill
There ye can play and drink your fill
D.D.D. J.J.

Locals hold that the three Ds after the verse signify either
Denis Died Drunk or Drink Drowned Denis, and argue at
great length as to the difference of meaning between the
two statements.

Of course, the Stone Fiddle did not always stand at the
entrance to Castlecaldwell. It was erected on the Rossagoale
shore, near the spot in the lake where the drowning took
place, where it was supported by two imposing limestone
columns. These were subsequently removed by a local stone-
mason who grafted them into gate pillars he was erecting for
a squireen close by. The fiddle he left leaning against the
gatehouse wall and it would most certainly have been chipped
away and carried off in small fragments had not the county's
antiquarian society, in their wisdom, come to the rescue and
had it cemented to the wall.

Sir James Caldwell had a museum at the Castle and among
his most treasured possessions was the skull of Turlough
O'Carolan, the celebrated harper and composer. It appears
that the bard's skull was stolen from its niche in the graveyard
of Kilronan, near Ballyfarnan, where O'Carolan was buried.
After many changes of ownership it was sold to Sir James
indirectly by a Ribbonman on the run for the sum of five
pounds.

After Sir James's day the skull found it's way to a most
select Orange Lodge in Belfast where it was accorded the
reverence shown to the Lia Fáil, the Stone of Destiny, once
used at Tara in the inauguration of the High King.

But back to Carolan and his skull. At the height of the cattle smuggling there was a famed flute player in the district named James McGinley, long since gone to garner grace notes within the golden gates of paradise. He struck up a rollicking reel-playing partnership with a local fiddler named Billy. One night, as they raced through a hurricane of reels, McGinley switched to that rare old tune, *Hand Me Down The Tacklings.*

The fiddler's thoughts took fire from the tune and: "Damn it! James", said he, "we'll run a heating of poteen ourselves for Hallow Eve." McGinley agreed that it was a holy and a wholesome thought, but where would they find a safe hide-out for distillation and the country crawling with customs men and police. Then they thought of the vaults under the old castle. It was an eerie spot, lonely and remote. They would be safe as meal in a chest there. There was an abundant supply of water to hand to keep the worm cool and it would be a simple matter to gather and store away enough drift-wood in the vaults to fuel the fire. As the vaults opened onto the lake, they would moor a boat nearby and slip away silently by water in the unlikely event of a raid.

Plans went ahead and the barrem was ripe and ready for running in good time for Hallow Eve. But fate intervened. An uncle died and had to be waked and buried, so that it was All Souls' Night before the two boyos got round to making their drop of the "craythur".

That particular night, while devout women and pious old men made visits to the church for the souls in Purgatory, our heroes set about releasing other spirits in the vaults of Castle-caldwell. It was very dark but windy enough to waft away any whiff or scent of the precious liquor that might escape at the mouth of the vaults during distilling operations.

The fire, kindled well back to the rear of the vaults, cast ghostly shadows along the walls but was completely screened by the stone arches and buttresses that supported the castle, and by a line of thick-set spruce that fringed the loughshore. The fiddler, who had been bothered with a new tune throughout the days of the wake and funeral, and dared not take down the fiddle to shape it in deference to the dead man, brought his "board" along that night to the stillhouse, where he could flake away without fear or hindrance.

About the murk and midnight hour, the first drops began to trickle through and as McGinley set a wooden keg under the snout of the worm, Billy reached for the fiddle and began tuning her. He had just finished his warming up .tune, *The Salamanca Reel*, when two strange figures crossed the threshold of light at the far end of the vaults. One of them wore a long, black cloak with a hood. The other sported a swallow-tail and knickerbockers.

McGinley's first impulse was to bolt past the strangers for it struck him that they might be police in disguise, but then, to his horror, he noticed that the man in the cloak had no head and the hood covered only a scrawny stump of a neck. He was petrified with fear. This was All Souls' Night. Could their visitors be from the other world?

Billy, on the other hand, launched out into a medley of reels and the swallow-tailed and knickerbockered one began to whistle the tunes along with him. "Do you play?" Billy made bold to ask, at the same time reaching him the fiddle. "I used to", came the reply, "but I haven't lifted a fiddle for years." He took the fiddle and retuned it. It was then the poteen makers heard *The Boys Of The Lough* played in a manner and with a plaintiveness that would draw tears from a stone and at the same time set every toe in the parish tapping.

"Can you play *Ceann Dubh Dílis?*" inquired the deep voice from the depth of the cloak.

"I learned it long ago from O'Hempsie one time he came to Castle Archdale", his companion told him, "I wonder can I recall it to memory." He played that hauntingly beautiful air and the two local musicians didn't know which end of them was up.

"Damn it! man, you're powerful", Billy blurted out, no longer able to contain his admiration, "you could draw music from the Stone Fiddle below at the gatehouse."

"No fiddler ever played on his tombstone", the stranger gave him back, and then a rooster crew down at Willie Green's.

"Come on, Terry, your skull is no longer here. If it was I'd have found it long ago. Keep McCabe's music alive, Billy. Good Night!" and their visitors vanished.

It was then the poteenmen twigged they had been listening to Caldwell's musician and jester. McGinley was frightened out of his wits and he didn't sober for days. Billy was forced to consult Big Pat O'Connor, the local scholar and historian, to establish the identity of their other visitor. When Pat told him that it could only be Turlough O'Carolan, the harper and last of the Bards: "Damn it!" commented Billy, with genuine regret, "why hadn't we a harp with us?"

"They'll see them in Newtownbutler when they waken to-morrow morning!" exclaimed Big Hughie as he glanced up at the new goal posts we had just settled into their sockets at Magherameena Park, the evening before the junior county championship final. A toss of the coin had decided the venue and so the re-organised Mulleek team found themselves hosting the final in which they were to do battle with far away Newtownbutler, the very first year of their re-entry into competitive Gaelic football. The new goal-posts were the pride of the local club and they drew grudging admiration even from the Gaels of Belleek.

These posts were cut on the Eagle Island and towed by a boat to the old Castle. They were then borne on the shoulders of the mighty Mulleek men to Magherameena Park, four miles away, where they now soared into the heavens as high as gulf light. The Mulleek team was indeed a band of giants. Out of the fifteen stalwarts who took the field on that historic Sunday, eleven were over six feet. They out-fielded, out-foxed and over-ran the boys from Newtownbutler, who may have been intimidated by the tall goalposts, for the fame of the sitka spruce that grew in the Leggs Wood nearby had gone further than Fermanagh. They were and still are the tallest timber in Western Europe.

The team was powered by three sets of brothers, the McGaurans, the O'Connors and the McCaffertys, with the help of the athletic and sky-raking Phillip Breen and the scheming and clever James McKeaney.

But, unquestionably, the greatest warrior of that star-studded side was Big Hughie McGauran, a magnificent specimen of manhood, standing in all his glory at six feet one inch, with a torso like Tarzan and a shot that shattered crossbars and uprights and swept away goalies, motor cars, ricks of hay or any other animate or inanimate thing that chanced to lie in the line of fire. It is doubtful if modern science has yet devised an instrument to measure the velocity of the ball as it blasted from his boot until it ripped through the netting at the back of the goal.

There was the famous day of the seven-a-side tournament at the back of Molly Garvin's in Belleek against the Ballyshannon men. Phillip Breen gave Hughie a ball going in on the twenty-one yard line and the big forward unleashed a piledriver. Arah man! sure they were the rest of the evening sawing the poor, unfortunate goalie out of the fork of an ash bush behind the goal and broke a cross-cut saw and the shafts of two hatchets in the operation. These were the days of the giants, the mighty men of yore!

Happily, Big Hughie McGauran is still with us, hale and hearty in the house he built with his own hands overlooking the Nore valley at Bennett's Bridge in Kilkenny. Even among the hurling heroes of the black and amber Red Branch Knights, Hughie is still the Conor Mac Nessa.

The morning throbs with thrushes's song
And life is shaken in a shout
From farming boy with trumpet throat
Who flutes a lip to fling a note
And hunts a thieving heifer out
As collie hanches at her heels
He lilts old rousing mountain reels
Replaces stones upon the ditch
And whistles home the barking bitch

Thrush song everywhere, flushing out the sullen silence of winter, filling the sun-soaked solitudes with seas of sound, welling out into the wilderness to the very edge of the bog-lark belt. And look! that bog is alive with larks cork-screwing song into the high dome of heaven.

The lark in the morning she rises off her nest
She goes up in the air with the dew on her breast
Like a jolly ploughboy she whistles and she sings
And comes home in the evenings with the dew on her wings.

Ploughboy did you say? No ploughshare ever turned the tiny fields the foothills wear as patches in their homespun: rocks and stones and fistfuls of clay.

Mountainy man with his cudding cows
Earth a bed and the spade his spouse.
Triumph he wins when the keeby knows
Snuggle their heads in a greener grass
Money wrung from the rocks bone-bare
Bargain clinched in the Lammas fair
Quickening pulse of a poet's prayer
Shortens his six-mile tramp to Mass.

And here on the green hill of Tullyhasson lived William Monaghan a troubadour whose like we seldom meet. William

38

had a wealth of songs. He was gone to God before my time but, so vividly did he stamp his image on the minds of the mountainy folk and so delightful are the stories and legends associated with his life amongst them, that I always regarded him as one of my dearest friends.

He had songs of love, religion and patriotism that did not seem to survive in any other part of the country. He sang a enchanting little song of hope and promised deliverance called *Erin The Green:*

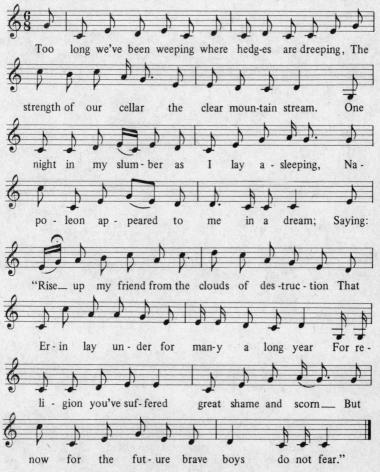

Refrain:
On the shores we did stand, where Napoleon did land
For he was the hero was longed to be seen
The bells of the chapel resounded a ditty
To welcome Napoleon to Erin The Green.

From hill and deep valleys, from mountains — our allies
The bells of old abbeys with joy that did peal
The Three Waves they thundered as we stood and wondered
And these are the words he would utter, I ween:
"O cead míle fáilte! my friend you are welcome
To raise up the shamrock in Erin The Green."

It was one of those special nights and William was in his
element. The dance was in the Ring, that is the first house on
Tamur Cassey, then owned by Pat Meehan, or Banks of
Dunmore Pat, as he was mostly called. Mary Gallagher of The
Mountain Streams had just finished that song and William's
reply was *Willie Reilly and his Dear Colleen Bán*. He sang the
whole of that beautiful and dramatic ballad and, my mother
told me, you could hear a pin drop throughout the performance:

O — rise — up Wil - lie Reil - ly, and come a- long with
me _____ I mean for to go with you, ____ and
leave — this count - er - ie _____ I'll leave my fa - ther's
cas - tle, ____ his ___ riches ___ and free lands And a - way —
went Wil - lie Reil - ly and his own dear Col-leen Ban. ___

O'er lofty hills and mountains, through silent groves and plains
Through shady groves and valleys, all danger to refrain
Her father followed after, with his well-armed band
And taken was poor Reilly and his own dear Colleen Ban

It's home then she was taken and in her closet bound
Poor Reilly all in Sligo jail lay on the stony ground
Till at the bar of justice before the judge he'd stand
For nothing but the taking of his own dear Colleen Ban

And now I'm in cold irons, my hands and feet are bound
I'm handcuffed like a murderer and tied unto the ground
But all this toil and slavery I'm willing for to stand
In hopes that I'll be succoured by my own dear Colleen Ban

The jailer's son to Reilly goes, and this to him did say
O rise up Willie Reilly, to stand your trial this day
The great Squire Folliard's anger you never can withstand
I fear you'll suffer sorely for your own dear Colleen Ban

This is the news O'Reilly, last night I heard of thee
The lady's oath will hang you, or else will set you free
If that be true, said Reilly, with pleasure I will stand
In hopes that I'll be succoured by my own dear Colleen Ban

Now Reilly's dressed from top to toe, all in a suit of green
His hair hangs o'er his shoulders, most glorious to be seen
He's tall and straight and comely as any could be found
He's fit for Folliard's daughter were she heiress to a crown

The judge he said this lady being in her tender youth
If Reilly has deluded her she will declare the truth
Then like a moving beauty bright before them she did stand
You're welcome there, my heart's delight, my own dear Colleen Ban

O gentlemen, Squire Folliard said, with pity look on me
This villain came amongst us to disgrace my family
And by his base contrivance this villainy was planned
I'll have the life of Reilly or I'll leave this Irish land

The lady all in tears began, and thus replied she
The fault is none of Reilly's, the blame is all on me
I forced him for to leave his place and come along with me
I loved all out of measure, which proved our destiny

Then out bespoke the noble Fox, at the table as he stood by
O gentleman, consider in this extremity
To hang a man for love is a murder you may see
So spare the life of Reilly to leave this counterie

Good my lord, he stole from her her jewels and her rings
Gold watch and silver buckles and many precious things
Which cost me in bright value above two thousand pounds
I'll have the life of Reilly or my estate I'll drown

Good my lord, I gave them all in token of true love
And now that we are parting, I'll have them all removed
If you have them O'Reilly pray send them back to me
I will, my loving lady, with many thanks, said he

There is one ring among them which I gave you to wear
With thirty diamond lockets, well set in silver hair
As a token of my true love, wear it on your right hand
That you may think on my broken heart, when in a foreign land

Then out bespoke the noble Fox, pray let the prisoner go
The lady's oath has cleared him, as the jury all do know
She has released her own true love and has renewed his name
That her honour great, may gain estate and everlasting fame

Pat himself was then called upon for *The Banks of Dunmore,* that ever popular confirmation of belief in the rectitude of the Old Faith:

You mai-dens of high and low sta-tion,—— And gent-le-men all of re-nown Give ear to—these few words I men-tion,—— The—truth I would like to pen down—— Con-cern-ing that beauti-ful dam-sel—— The heart from my— bo-som she tore—— And she's on-ly a— poor far-mer's daugh-ter.—— —— Who lives on the Banks of Dun-more.——

The hair that hangs over her shoulders
Like ringlets of gold on her head
Her skin is as white as the lilly
And her cheeks they bloom a rosy red
The more I gaze on that fond creature
The longer I wished to delay
The heart she has plucked from my bosom
And with her has stolen it away

At length I approached this fond female
Saying my dear will you tell me your name
If you're of the Christian creation
Won't you tell me from whence, love, you came
For I am a man of great title
Of riches and great earthly store
And tonight I will make you my equal
And live on the Banks of Dunmore.

Kind sir, we're not of one persuasion
The truth I will tell you indeed
I'm of the Christian creation
And ruled by the Catholic creed
The Scriputre I oftimes peruse it
And God I did take for my guide
Until that you do turn a Roman
You shall never have me for your bride.

Fair maid, I will start you one question
Explain it to me if you can
The Bible's the guide of our Religion
And how can you prove that I'm wrong
But if you confute me by Scripture
My parents I'll always disown
And with you I'll become a true member
And live up to your true Church of Rome

Kind sir, it is an easy matter
To prove unto you that you're wrong
Transubstantiation we believe in
You'll find it in the Book of John
And if that you want to go further
Sure God he made Peter his own
The keys of his treasure he gave him
To govern the true Church of Rome.

In hopes that we may have a blessing
This night from the heavens above
Controversy we'll freely abolish
And join in the arms of love
Your grand explanation has won me
My dear I will make you my own
And with you I'll become a true member
And live up to the true Church of Rome.

When the applause had died away, William flung his hat on the floor and declared he'd sing *The Song of Temptation:*

When the small birds of the ou - ter air, They sport with one an -

oth - er, Then why should you and me — de - fer to —

sport all gay — to - geth- er? Good mu - sic, sir, would

make one dance Un - less their limbs would fail —— them I

fear your wear some damp must bear Or — sure - ly you'd re -

veal them With me did-dery dum a-da, with my did-dery dum

a da With me did-de - ry dum a dad- dle dee a di - deo.

For naked we came on this earth
And naked we'll go under
So why wear clothes, and costly hose
To hide the heights of wonder
Great Adam when he wooed his Eve
No ring she wore or diamond
But naked they did sport and play
All round the Horn of Hymen.

O maiden fair with me forbear
Don't talk with tongue of fire
For Holy Writ will never quit
To purge us of desire
For chastity's a beacon bright
That beams throughout the ages
To guide us on the darkest night
When the storm of passion rages.

Since free will is a gift divine
For man's emancipation
Free love's a draught of Cupid's wine
To tease us with temptation
For laws and rules were made for fools
Each day they're getting stricter
So come with me, we'll sport in glee,
Let Venus be the victor.

When David turned from God and grace
No armies did applaud him
And none were saved in that depraved
And sinful city Sodom
And look you then to storied Troy
What led to it's destruction?
But vengeances for vice of rape
And ravishing seduction.

King Solomon, that monarch wise
Wooed thrice three hundred lovers
He had wives and queens and concubines
The Scripture it uncovers
Let curving breasts be your fond quests
And yield to female charms
And lie one long and lusty night
All naked in my arms.

Begone you slut! Heaven is shut
To all such fornicators
To strumpets, whores and harlots all,
Likewise abominators
Matrimony was God's command
And matrimonial station
Without ado they then withdrew
This was their conversation.

When the thunder of applause had died down and Mary of The Mountain Streams had nudged William to his supreme effort with her jaunty little song, *Wee Paddy Molloy,* he wound up the evening's entertainment with *The Redemption Song,* in which the Creation, the Fall and Redemption were portrayed in one grand sweep. *(Tune: Bean dubh an ghleanna.)*

> Good people great and small, of any faith at all
> Come gather round and listen to my story
> Concerning God above, the abundance of his love
> Our Creator and All-Mighty King of Glory
> The Commandment from on high was increase and multiply
> And spread throughout the earth and every nation
> Our first parents they obeyed, then their innocence did trade
> For a mess of potage, death and desolation.
>
> Driven forth from Eden fair by the Serpent's cunning snare
> Looking back, the flaming sword they still saw turning
> Adam toiled and Eve she span and begot the sons of man
> All through bitter sweat and blood and sore heart-burning.
> Hard beset by mortal fears they traversed the Vale of Tears
> For the heritage of Heaven they had squandered
> But a Saviour would be sent, if for sin they would repent
> Twas the promise that sustained them as they wandered.
>
> On that cold December morn when the Son of God was born
> All the men of Mammon spurned him as a stranger
> Though he came their souls to win, there was no room at the inn
> So his mother, Mary laid him in a manger.
> Heaven's angels spread the news and glad tidings to the Jews
> That a King was born the force of sin to sunder
> And the Magi saw the Star and they followed from afar
> And they knelt in awe and worshipped him with wonder
>
> When he grew to man's estate and the Good News did relate
> All the leprous, blind and lame came forth to hear him;
> For he healed their hearts of strife and the dead were raised to life;
> He forgave the sinners great who did draw near him.
> But the chief priests and the scribes, by foul means and falser bribes,
> Sought to undermine the tenets of his teaching.
> But the truth he did expound and their sages did confound
> When in temple or on mountain he was preaching.

As an earnest of his task he would eat with them the Pasch;
The Apostles would remember his example
But the crowds that gathered round spread palm branches on the
        ground
As in triumph he rode forward to the Temple
Though with one voice they did sing loud hosannas to the their King
Still he knew that Peter soon was to deny him
In the space of six short days they would change from songs of praise
To the shouts of crucify him! crucify him!

Father let thy will be done, was the cry of God's own Son,
As he sweated blood to win us sinners pardon
In that dark before the day he was seized and led away
Judas did his lord betray all in the Garden
Then false testimony they bore and high-priests their garments tore
And reviled him with their wicked, bitter scorning
For thirty pieces he was sold, as the Scripture does unfold,
And convicted on a Good Friday morning.

Jesus Christ was crucified and between two thieves he died
As the earth it shook and rocks were rent asunder.
And his scoffers fell in fright as the noon became the night
While the Roman soldiers watched in awe and wonder.
But in three short days he rose, all triumphant o'er his foes
And redeemed us all from death and desolation;
Now we're safe from Satan's wrath, on the straight and narrow path
That will lead us home to Heaven and our Salvation.

In the townland of Rusheen lived Johnnie Hump McGee, gamekeeper, crank and bitter cynic. When my mother, God rest her, was at school he seized the makings of a heather besom from her that she had plucked in the Demesne. The Demesne was a small grove of trees that grew on the banks of Lough Suaimhneach near the mouth of the Tullyvogie road. It has long since been cut down. In those days it was famed for it's bilberry bushes but if Hump found the school children next or near the luscious blue-black berries he scutched the legs off them with a long, black sally rod.

They will tell you in those mountainy parts that Johnnie McGee was once as straight as a yard of pumped water until the night the stray came on him at the back of Breen Mountain.

It appears Johnnie was gathering his small flock of sheep on the southern side of the mountain one October evening when all of a sudden, a thick mist rolled up from marshy moorland below, and in the clapping of your hands he couldn't see his finger before him. Night fell and he was still astray. He was frightened for he knew well there was a stray on that same mountain. So he took off his coat, cut the Sign of the Cross on himself and put on the coat again inside out. At once he recognised a grey rock the sheep used for rump scratching. As he approached, a door opened in the rock face to let a shaft of light fall out on the heather.

Johnnie stepped over the threshold and into a long, narrow corridor hewn out of rock. It was lighted by blazing torches of bog-oak struck into iron brackets along the wall. He followed his nose for there was a pleasant aroma of cooking meat coming from the further end of the passage. Presently, he came to a heavy oaken door. As he approached, the door

swung open and a friendly voice bade him welcome to the
Land of Fey.

Before him was a long, rectangular room well lighted with
torches and, at the far end, sat the fairy king and queen on
high thrones. In no time at all Johnnie was seated at table
near the thrones enjoying the feasting and fun of the banquet. As soon as he emptied his flagon it was refilled with the
most wonderful liquor he had ever tasted. Johnnie reckoned
that it must have been mead.

As he heartily drank the healths of the king and queen
he observed twenty hairy hunchbacks perched on high har-
rowpins that protruded from the walls on either side. Their
faces were distorted in the most hideous grins and their general
bearing was one of malevolence. A shudder ran through
Johnnie as though someone was walking over his grave.

The banquet was followed by song and dance and the
sweetest music that ever soothed mortal ear. Although he
was feeling the effects of the liquor he distinctly heard the
command issued with the snuff as it was passed around, not
to invoke the name of the Almighty if a sneeze escaped a
snuffer.

A habit is hard to break, and when Johnnie partook of the
snuff and duly sneezed, his loud invocation to his creator to
bless him froze the laughter and merriment on the features of
the fairy host.

"Johnnie McGee", roared the king, now livid with rage,
"you have abused the hospitality of your host. There is only
one penalty for such a transgression, the penalty of death!"
But the fairy queen, who had taken a strong fancy to Johnnie,
pleaded for clemency, and at length the king relented. Johnnie
would not be put to death. Instead the king commanded his
warriors to take down the twenty hunchbacks off their harrow-
pins and tramp the twenty humps off them and unto the
broad back of Johnnie McGee! And it was done.

Then there was sudden darkness. The walls of the banquet
hall fell away and Johnnie and the fairy host were out in the
swirling mists of the mountainside.

"Bring me my steed", shouted the fairy king, and at once he mounted and rode away into the night.

"Bring me my steed", called the fairy queen and just as quickly she was mounted and rode after him.

"Give me a horse", shouted each warrior in turn and immediately he was mounted and galloped off.

"Give me a horse", Johnnie made bold to ask, and a fine prancing stallion stood before him. He sprang to the saddle and joined the Slua Shee in their headlong gallop over the bogs and moors of Ireland.

When it cleared daylight in the morning Johnnie McGee was straddle-legged on a whin bush at the back of his own house, his rump like a pin-cushion with sharp whin spikes.

He thanked God for delivering him from the fairy host, but feeling the weight on his back, put round his hand. It was too true. The horrible hump was there, weary and woeful as the heap of sin that weighs down the world.

"In the name of God, where does he come from?" inquired the wirey, old woman as she smacked away on the shank of her clay dudeen, the toothless mouth tightening in round the pipe stem like a drawing-string purse.

"From behind God's speed where the devil foaled the fiddler", Big Johnnie gave her back.

"He's no foal him, leastways a devil's foal!" she bantered.

"He's a fiddler all the same", the big man teased her.

"Troth and you can say that again, and as good as ever drew a bow!" she added, "but tell us now, Johnnie dear, where does he come from?"

"He's a Toura man", Johnnie told her, "and a Protestant to boot", in a tone of finality that brooked no further questions.

"A Protestant fiddler!" she exclaimed incredulously, "that beats fighting cocks! But then they say there is such a fowl as a white blackbird, and from Toura!" And she burst into song:

> Toura for sour buttermilk
> Belleek for the brandy
> The Commons was the divil's hole
> But Mulleek was the dandy.

She sang in highland fling time, oblivious of the dark musician who graced and ornamented *The Fermoy Lasses* with all the delicacy and dedication of a craftsman in the flowering shop of Belleek Pottery.

That was my first meeting with John Cowan at the home of Johnnie the Jeweller in Dernacross. For Johnnie did not confine his talents to watches and clocks. He also mended wheezy, asthmatic, old melodeons and balanced the governors of gramophones. Indeed he could fit those great and glorious machines with main springs and any other part they might require.

I had arrived with a gramophone that needed a new main spring, strapped on my back, and walked straight into a hurricane of reels that raced from the bow of the big boney fiddler from the "Bar of Wee Alt."

Francey Bell Keown was next to darken the door of that meeting-house of music lovers and he bore on his back a wooden box of the latest traditional gramophone records. These included Michael Coleman, Hughie Gillespie, Paddy Kiloran and James Morrison. Cowan could speak with authority on the relative and absolute merits of all four masters. He greatly admired Coleman's playing but Gillespie he regarded as God's gift to mankind.

Francey Bell could whistle like the blithest blackbird that ever piped on hawthorn bough, but his lilting was the most melodious I have ever heard. He could dance a reel-hornpipe with the best step dancers beyond the lough, but seemed to be under the shadow of that grand old troubadour, Pat Bell Keown, his father, when it came to singing.

When John Cowan put the fiddle back in the case we veted a number of the records on the repaired gramophone. I was in a quandry. I had only the price of one record, which was one shilling and nine pence at the time. Which one should I take? Coleman's *Bonnie Kate* or Gillespie's *Master Crowley's Reels?* Eventually I settled for the Gillespie tunes in the hope that my sister Maureen would salvage the price of *Bonnie Kate* from her next fortnight's pay packet.

Cowan and myself cycled back together as far as Rosscor, but before we parted he promised to come over to us for a night's fiddling before Christmas.

I remember well the night he came. Brian McGuire from The Dogs, near Derrygonnelly, was with him and together they made it as far as Flanagan's in Tierygannon, and Billy, who used to ceili to our house at the time, brought them the rest of the way.

It was a Saturday night and, altogether against the run of the mill, Jady Ward and Mick Hernon dropped in around night-

falling. Jady was the fiddler at that time and Mick played the
melodeon. Word was sent down to O'Connor's for Mary Ellen
and Hughie, and Jimmie Cox, a clinking reel-dancer who lived
next door, was contacted.

It was a mighty night's music and dancing with the odd
song thrown in for good measure but the greatest excitement
was generated by the contrasting styles of the fiddle players.
The fiddlers from beyond the lough played music you would
like to listen to, we decided, but the Mulleek fiddlers made
you dance. I am sure it was the memory of Denis McCabe
and the image of the great Stone Fiddle that inspired them to
the heights reached that night. And sure as shooting, from
that night onwards, Mick Hernon abandoned the open reed
instrument and devoted all his talents and spare time to the
fiddle.

There was a snatch of a song that Cowan and McGuire sang
along with their fiddle music for one part of the lancers. It
went like this:

> John James O'Hara, and Mickey McNamara
> O they are famous Irishmen no matter where they go
> They are known for their doin's
> They are men of great influence
> O'Hara from Tara, McNamara from Mayo.

> Now that we're returning back to dear old Erin's Isle
> Back to home and plenty after many a weary mile
> To the heather on the hillside
> And the sunshine down below
> O'Hara from Tara, McNamara from Mayo.

It added liveliness and laughter to the dance. When Mick
Hernon, still one of Castlecaldwell's great fiddle-players, was
in good spirit and flaking that fine jig, *The Rakes of Kildare,*
he invariably broke into song:

> As I was going into the fair of Athy
> I spied an oul' petticoat hanging up high
> I took off my trousers and hung them up high
> To keep that old petticoat warm

The petticoat fluttered, and made a loud noise
It lifted it's tail and lost feminine poise
And all round it's flounces it wrapped my corduroys
Old trousers I hope you're in form.

The night of the wedding, the night of the fun
The night of the wedding she had a big son
The father is dead, he was shot with a gun
And the neighbours maintained 'twas no harm.

John Cowan and myself remained firm friends and great lovers of the music of Coleman and Gillespie. When the war broke out he joined the Merchant Navy and I have not seen him since. I am told he is still alive and well but where, I do not know. He was a fine musician and one of nature's gentlement. Maybe we shall meet again.

When I finished school in Derryhallow, where myself and another boy were hopelessly in love with the handsome young female Principal, my course was set for Ballyshanny on the winding banks of Erne where, at the vocational school, a wry old bachelor from Oughterdrum told me that headsheaf would be put on my learning. In those days, before the second World War upset the equilibrium of human nature, there was no talk of first level, second level or third level education.

Aristotle's dictum that all men are actuated by a desire for knowledge held sway, so that instead of education levels there were heights of learning to be scaled. Moreover there were no pupils or students. Such names are good enough for post-war plebians one supposes, but we rejoiced in the noble title of *scholar,* be we at national school or vocational academy.

The problem of transport was quickly resolved. I had just earned my first quarter's salary as local correspondent for *The Donegal Democrat,* and the good editor had sent me a cheque for seventeen shillings and sixpence. Paddy Keenan was bound for Scotland the Brave to push his fortune and his iron horse was on the market. He'd take a paper pound for the machine. I made him an offer of a ten shilling note. He wouldn't hear tell of it. In the heel of the hunt, after a good deal of haggling and hand-clapping, the price was made at thirteen shillings and sixpence, with a luck penny of one silver shilling. Micky Monaghan tightened up the brakes and adjusted the chain, for I was never the handiest of men with machinery. Micky assured me that we'd now be able to go to dances in far off Finnaduss and Tullyluskin, where the women were wild about strange men. Micky was older than I and worked hard in quarries, drawing out limestone for road metal with a shaggy-maned horse and a heavy trundling cart. He owned a sparkling new Raleigh bicycle that was his pride and joy and the envy of boys like me with our twelve and sixpenny machines. What pleased me, even more than the thoughts of romance with the eager women of Finnaduss, was the fact that I still had money enough left from my journalistic earning to pay the fee, of five shillings, for the right to drink for one year at the fount of knowledge that was Ballyshanny technical school.

So, one fine September morning, I mounted my iron horse and set off in search of learning to Ballyshanny. Nothing of note happened as I passed through the village of Belleek until I pedalled on up the brae beyond the customs hut towards Cookey McCauley's.

There, before me on the road, her shapely limbs propelling a bicycle in the same direction as myself was the the spéirbhean that was to haunt my sleeping and waking hours for many years to come. No raven's plume could match the coal-black sheen of her hair, nor could the most deadly darts of Cupid ravish man's soul with such unutterable pain and passion as a glance from her big brown eyes.

She wore a plaited skirt and a tight-fitting blouse under which the rythmic rise and fall of her bosom was like the swell of billows on a wine-dark sea. She rode alone. Filled with the most noble thoughts of chivalry and the zeal of the knights of old, I spurred my iron horse and hastened to her side.

Then mutual love together drew us without a fond embrace. Indeed the only physical contact throughout our years of wonderful Platonic love was my hand on her shoulder as we cycled along the country road. In truth such lustless love was, like the heroes who rode with Count O'Hanlon, of the spirit stuff. O Josephine! What a holy and wholesome relationship was ours. The thoughts of youth are long, long thoughts.

In the school on the Mall, overlooking famed Assaroe, we gathered to garner wisdom and learning. Perhaps that renowned waterfall, long since blasted to oblivion by the predators who masquerade under the mantle of progress, was the finest teacher we ever had.

All day long the waters fumed and thundered over the sheer face of the Fall, to rainbow out in rays of radiant colour over the foaming pool below. Downstream, towards the island of Innish Samer, where Partholan was the first man to set foot on the green sward of Ireland, the salmon lay so thick that they formed a silver causeway across to the other bank. One of their number could easily have been Bradán Easa Aodh Ruaidh or the Salmon of Assaroe itself, famed far and near for wit and wisdom, although it was only three hundred years of age.

The scholar who had a knotty problem to unravel, was invariably advised to seek the aid of the Salmon. If the Salmon's memory faltered, he was instructed to proceed to the Crow of Achill or Préachán Acla, a creature twice as old and possessed of a double degree of knowledge. If both these sages failed to find an answer to the riddle there was only one hope left. That was, of course, an appeal to the Cailleach Béara, or the Hag of Bere, whose age was thrice three hundred years and whose wisdom bested that of Solomon.

The waterfall derived it's name from Aodh Rua, warring chief of the early Celts, who was drowned crossing the Erne above the Falls. His more illustrious daughter, Macha Mong Rua, or Macha of The Red Mane, is better known in our Ulster of today. By cunning female stratagem, she captured her enemies and forced them to build Eamhain Macha, the Navan Fort, outside Armagh by slave labour. She was also Ireland's first nurse. A somewhat elongated bronze figure of this famous Ulster queen guards the grounds of Altnagelvin hospital near Colm's sainted city of Derry.

It was at this spot too, tradition tells us, Máire Chionnaith, that strange mixture of mermaid and landgirl, lay resting her limbs after swimming the breadth of the Erne. Her feat and fate is enshrined for ever in that poignantly beautiful Gaelic song, *An Mhaighdeán Mhara:*

Is cosúil gur mheath tú nó gur thréig tú an ghreann
Tá an sneachta go frasach fá bhéal na trá
Do chúl buí daite is do bhéil ín shámh
Siúd chugaibh Máire Chionnaith is í i ndiaidh an Éirne a shnámh

A mháithrín mhilis dúirt Máire bhán
Fá bhruach an chladaigh is fá bhéal na trá
Maighdeán mhara mo mháithrín ard,
Siúd chugaibh Máire Chionnaith is í i ndiaidh an Éirne a shnámh.

Tá mise tuirseach, agus beidh go lá
Mo Mháire bhruinneall is mo Phádraigh bán
Ar bharr na dtonna is fa bhéal na trá
Siud chugaibh Máire Chionnaith is í i ndiaidh an Éirne a shámh.

Next in importance as a teacher was Miss Hilda O'Boyle, who taught English and commerce. Why had such mundane and mercenary objects as self-balancing ledgers and bulky cash books to invade a cultured and cultivated mind like that of Miss Hilda?

Her love and appreciation of good literature was infectious.

The moan of doves in immemorial elms
The murmur of innumerable bees.

She declaimed Tennyson with an engaging charm and generally read poetry rather well for one with a lisp almost as pronounced as any English nun. She had a weakness for the romantic poetry of Yeats and those wonderful dreams he spread under the feet of Maude Gonne. At this point I invariably cast sidelong glances in the direction of the Black-Haired Lass across the classroom. I'd have spread myself under her feet just then.

Miss Hilda lent me Tolstoy's *Resurrection,* which I devoured with considerable relish, although I must confess to mild outrage when the flourish of strumpets made their entrance. The word prostitute was almost as detestable as that of Protestant in those enlightened days!

I recall an evening in late May after a Departmental examination. Released from the baleful stare of the supervisor, we hurried down the Mall where an open air céilí was in full swing. They were dancing a sixteen-hand reel to the tune of the *Dashing White Sergeant,* played on the fiddle by a tall slender, red-haired female. Fishermen were landing their catch. The salmon gleamed in the nets like silver scimitars. A sickle of a moon, golden as a sovereign, looked down out of a southern sky. We danced and were bewitched. At dusk we cycled home through hedges of blossomed hawthorn and a flutter of moth-wings, my hand on the shoulder of the Black-Haired Lass. I left her in Belleek and overtook Hughie O'Connor going out the Commons.

"The whitethorns are in full bloom. We'll have a mighty hatch of fly tomorrow", he declared.

"The big ones will be taking", I rejoined, feigning enthusiasm. But we had danced under a golden sickle of a moon and were bewitched.

12. ROOM, ROOM MY GALLANT ROOM

It was round November, when the nights were long, that dances, raffles and card-plays began to be held in the rambling houses of the loughside. There were two, or possibly three, great schools of twenty-five players in the district but no speech was allowed while the game was in progress.

The high spirits of the younger men did not take too kindly to the tyranny of silence imposed by the elders, and so we mitched from the stern card-playing schools and decided to go mumming.

We met at a rambling house frequented by traditional dancers and storytellers and rehearsals began. The designing of the costumes gave us great scope for invention, for the more grotesque and outlandish the apparel worn, the greater the welcome and enthusiasm extended us in the houses and homes where we performed.

The rhymes were easy to learn. Indeed most of us had already picked them up from the folklore and yarns of the storytellers. Our Mummers' Play ran as follows:

Room
Room, room, my gallant room, give me room to rhyme
I'll show you some activity about this Christmastime
The active youth, the active age
Our act was never acted on the stage
And if you don't believe these words I say
Enter in the Captain and he'll clear the way.

The Captain
Here comes I, the Captain, Captain of this noble crew.
Many great deeds I will relate to you.
My ship has ploughed the seven says
And now she's home to quiet bays
And if you don't believe these words I say
Enter in Oliver Cromwell and he'll clear the way.

Oliver Cromwell
Here comes I, Oliver Cromwell, with my long, copper nose
I have conquered many nations, as you may suppose
I made the French for to tremble and the Spanish for to quake
And I beat the jolly Dutchman, and made his heart ache.
And if you don't believe these words I say
Enter in Jack Straw and he'll clear the way.

Jack Straw
Here comes I, Jack Straw, such a man you never saw.
Through a rock, through a reel, through an old spinning wheel
Through a bag of pepper, through an old mill hopper
My mother was Straw, my father was Straw, why the hell wouldn't
    I be Straw.
And if you don't believe these words I say
Enter in Beelzebub and he'll clear the way

Beelzebub
Here comes I, Beelzebub, over my shoulder I carry my club
And in my hand a frying-pan, I think myself a jolly old man.
And if you don't believe these words I say
Enter in Never Came Yit and he'll clear the way.

Never Came Yit
Here comes I, Never Came Yit, big head and little wit
My head is big and my body small, I'll do my best to serve you all
And if you don't believe these words I say
Enter in Wee Divil Doubt and he'll clear the way

Wee Divil Doubt
Here comes I, Wee Divil Doubt
If I don't get money I'll clear you all out
Money I want, money I crave
If I don't get money, I'll sweep you all to the grave.
Five shillings, no less, all silver no brass
And if you don't believe these words I say
Enter in the The Wran, and he'll clear the way.

The Wran
Here comes I, the Wran, the Wran, the king of all birds
At Christmastime I was found in the furze
Although I am small my family is great
Rise up landlady and give me your trate

And if your trate is of the best
I hope your soul in Heaven will rest
But if your trate is very small
It won't agree with me at all
And if you don't believe these words I say
Enter in Prince George and he'll clear the way.

Prince George
Here comes I, Prince George, from England I have sprung
Many's the great an noble deed I've done
And valour to begin.
Seven long years in a close cave I've been kept
And out of that into a prison I lept
And out of that into a rock of stone
Where I made many a sad and grievous moan
Many a giant I did subdue
And many a fiery dragon slew
Now here I draw my courageous hand
Show me the man who would dare me stand.

Turkish Champion
I am the Turkish Champion, from Turkeyland I come
I'm one of the greatest champions in all Christendom
I am the man who now before you stand
Who you could not cut down with your fiery brand
Or your courageous hand.

Prince George
What are you but a poor stable boy
Who fed King Charlie's horse on oats and hay
For seven long years and then ran away

Turkish Champion
I say, Prince George, you lie, sir.

Prince George
Take out your sword and try sir.

Turkish Champion
(lunging at Prince George)
I drive my sword right through your heart
And cause you for to die, sir.
(Prince Geroge falls to the ground mortally wounded)

Captain
A Doctor, a doctor, five pounds for a doctor!

Doctor Brown
Yes, yes, I'm coming. Here comes I, Doctor Brown
The very best doctor in the town

Captain
What can you cure Doctor?

Doctor Brown
I can cure the plague within, the plague without.
The ague, the palzy or the gout.

Captain
What's your medicine Doctor?

Doctor Brown
The rue, the sue, the knuckles of a bumbee, the heart's blood of a
smoothing iron, all boiled up together.
And mixed with a black, buck-cat's feather.
I have a wee bottle in my inside, outside, upper
waistcoat pocket, called hokerous pokerous elegant pain
Rise up dead man, and fight again.

Prince George rises, restored to life and health.

Captain
Horrible! horrible! was the like ever seen
A man of seven senses driven into seventeen
By a buck, by a bear, by the devil's own ancestor's son and heir.

All Mummers join hands and sing together.

We'll join our hands together and never fight no more
We'll be as loyal comrades as we have been before
We'll bless the master of this house, and the mistress too
And all the little children who round the table grew
With their pockets full of money and their glasses full of beer
I wish you a merry Christmas and a bright New Year.

Captain
Sing boys sing!

Tam Brown
Let the king take the queen and the queen take the knave
We are a jolly company of stalwarts stout and brave
Here's to you Tam Brown, here's to you with all my heart
We'll have another glass or two this night before we part
Here's to you, Tam Brown.

The queen takes the knave and the knave takes the ten
We are a gallant company of strong and sturdy men
Here's to you Tam Brown, here's to you with all my heart
We'll have another glass or two this night before we part
Here's to you Tam Brown.

The knave takes the ten and the ten takes the nine
And since we're all together boys, good health to yours and mine
Here's to you Tam Brown, here's to you with all my heart
We'll have another glass or two this night before we part
Here's to you Tam Brown.

Let the ten take the nine and the nine take the eight
We are a jolly company of heroes tall and straight
Here's to you Tam Brown, here's to you with all my heart
We'll have another glass or two this night before we part
Here's to you Tam Brown.

Let the nine take the eight and the eight take the seven
And since we are together boys I think we'll head for heaven
Here's to you Tam Brown, here's to you with all my heart
We'll have another glass or two this night before we part
Here's to you Tam Brown.

Let the eight take the seven and the seven take the six
And when the drinking's over boys we'll hobble home on sticks
Here's to you Tam Brown, here's to you with all my heart
We'll have another glass or two this night before we part
Here's to you Tam Brown.

Let the seven take the six and the six take the five
And since we're all together boys we'll keep the fun alive
Here's to you Tam Brown, here's to you with all my heart
We'll have another glass or two this night before we part
Here's to you Tam Brown.

Let the six take the five and the five take the four
And since we're all together boys, we'll rap and call for more
Here's to you Tam Brown, here's to you with all my heart
We'll have another glass or two this night before we part
Here's to you Tam Brown.

Let the five take the four and the four take the tray
We are a jolly company, we'll drink till break of day
Here's to you Tam Brown, here's to you with all my heart
We'll have another glass or two this night before we part
Here's to you Tam Brown.

The four takes the tray and the tray takes the deuce
And since we're all together boys we'll drink the barley juice
Here's to you Tam Brown, here's to you with all my heart
We'll have another glass or two this night before we part
Here's to you Tam Brown.

The tray takes the deuce and the deuce takes the ace
We are a jolly company all full of fun and grace
Here's to you Tam Brown, here's to you with all my heart
We'll have another glass or two this night before we part
Here's to you Tam Brown.

Let the deuce take the ace and the ace take them all
And since we're all together boys, we'll make another call
Here's to you Tam Brown, here's to you with all my heart
We'll have another glass or two this night before we part
Here's to you Tam Brown.

Captain makes his call
Lady Grey, O Lady Grey, where have you wandered to this day.

Lady
Yes, yes I'm coming. Here comes I, Lady Grey
To dance your woes and cares away.

*She dances a traditional two-hand reel with the Captain, to fiddle
or melodeon music. The dance brings the Mummers' play to an end.*

I mind well one night we were mumming in Tullychurry. The
winter floods had so swollen the streams and watercourses
that those of us wearing boots or shoes had to be ferried
across the fords on the shoulders of the wellingtoned brigade.
My brother Joe, who was a lightly built short-trousered boy
of twelve years at the time, was borne on the broad back of
Packie Lawn for most of the way. You see he was our musician and rattled out rousing reels on the old fashioned melodeon with the three stoppers.

It was a delicate area for us to work as the inhabitants

were entirely Protestant, and very strict in their observance
of the proprieties. However, they did have an Orange Hall
and a jaunty little fife and drum band and perhaps this preserved a tiny oasis of culture in somewhat arid surroundings.
Maybe it was for that reason they gave us such a royal welcome and we in turn made sure that we visited every house
and acted our play on every hearthstone in that townland.

The women in most of the houses there, both young and
old, indulged in a little judicious levity when we entered. One
never could decide whether it was our exotic costumes or the
sudden invasion of their kitchen floors by so many virile
young men that excited them. Whatever the reason for the
strange behaviour, Oliver Cromwell and Turkish Knight were
lucky to escape without their high and handsome headgear
getting three or four belts of the brushy end of a broom
wielded by one or other of these wild Tullychurry women.

However, it was the entry of Wee Divil Doubt, who sported
the horns of the biggest buck-goat Paul McCabe ever kept
in stud, that drove them out of their senses altogether. A
female emerged from the shadows to grab a horn in every
hand and when he chased her playfully round the house and
dunted her in the hindquarters with his powerful antlers,
she howled hilariously.

Another night we were mumming in Derrarona and I had
the role of Prince George. Hughie O'Connor, revelling in the
part of Turkish Knight, cut me down on cue. I duly fell to
the floor mortally wounded but failed to see the heap of
dung built up by the droppings of a bull calf tied in the
corner, as my visor was down. I was amazed when my slayer
kicked me gently in the ribs and bade me, in a loud whisper
to get up to hell out of that:

"But I can't! The doctor hasn't arrived to bring me round."

"Better rowl over into the middle of the floor then, or
you'll be drowned in a flood of calf's piss."

The summer of nineteen thirty-nine was one of fear and foreboding. Hitler was at his old capers again in Europe and old-timers like Tommie's Johnnie and Biddy's Edward, who had sojourned for long spells in Scotland as tatty-hokers and turnip toppers and tailers, talked endlessly of war and the rumours of war. Old prophecies were looked up and quoted at great length round the hearths of the ceili houses where we gathered and Johnnie Denis reminded us that the old people maintained the war would come between mowing and reaping time or scythe and sickle time. Idir speal agus corrán a thiocfas an cogadh.

War was declared and work became plentiful. We were encouraged to plant more potatoes and oats and to "dig for victory". The marginal land that had been reclaimed from cut-away bog was no place for the ploughshare, so the spade, known in our part of the country as the McMahon, after the name of the manufacturer, was most in demand. The subsidy for breaking lea was two pounds per acre, to which was added a further ten pounds in the autumn when the crop was harvested.

I can assure you that a lot of sweat went into that sour and sullen soil before the twelve pounds were earned. However, the potato yields were mostly good and the quality excellent, which is more than can be said for the potato crops in those parts today. "A basin of good Kerr's Pinks is meat and kitchen for a king", the old people used to say. Perhaps it was this regard for the potato that led to the snatch of a song known as *Mary Anne McGuigan:*

"Are your pritties dry or are they fit for diggin'?"
"Take your spade and try, O Mary Anne McGuigan!"
"You'll spray them spuds again; that field the Pinks grow big in"
"You've bluestone on the brain, O Mary Anne McGuigan!"

Chorus
Mary Anne McGware, at the porter she was swiggin'
She'd shame you I declare, says Mary Anne McGuigan

John James he led the dance, with his jazzin' and his jiggin'
Retire and then advance and swing with Miss McGuigan
He drunk her buttermilk from a noggin and a piggin
And bought a blouse of silk for Mary Anne McGuigan.

Chorus
Her roof's the worse of wear, from the eave up to the riggin'
But who'll put up a spar for Mary Anne McGuigan
Her haggard holds the straw, where the stacks stand trim and trig in
"I'll thresh your oats and draw them, Mary Anne McGuigan!"

Chorus
There was another delightful little ditty involving the tuber
introduced by Raleigh. It was sung to the tune of *The Stack
of Barley,* that set-dance immortalised by the maestro Michael
Coleman. Here it is:

Did you ever see the Divil, with his wooden leg and shovel
Digging pritties in the garden with his tail cocked up
When the flies they started fizzin' sure that tail around went whizzin'
But they dragged him back to prison, where he's now locked up.

To the Divil's great delight, sure the spuds got black with blight. .
And the people died all frightened of the famine and the woe.
But Saint Patrick taught him manners, and upset the foreign planners
He re-grew the Pinks and Banners in the fields both high and low.

The foreign planners was a reference to the British policy in
Ireland during the Great Hunger of black forty-seven.

The coping or sousing of an acre of lea, when the keen cutting edge of the McMahon was thrust through rush roots and
keeby knowes with more force than was really necessary,
caused every muscle and bone of the body to ache for a week
of Sundays. No wonder the song said: "and the County Fermanagh for muscle and bone". Both were needed to break
the grey begrudging soil of the drumlins or the soggy peat of
the moorland.

One evening in June, as Joe and myself were toiling away
breaking tough fibred moss in the furrows between the ridges

to make potato moulding, Johnnie McGoldrick threw his leg
over the stone fence on Seanbhaile and invited me to become
a timber-feller in the Castlecaldwell demesne. I accepted the
invitation in welcome.

So began my career in the woods along the loughshore.
Norway had fallen to Hitler and the supply of pit-props for
the coalmines of Great Britain had been cut off. Our task was
to assist in providing an alternative supply. The first stage in-
volved only thinnings. The trees were felled and slipped or
carried to depots along the road that ran through the woods,
to await the arrival of the power-driven buzz-saw, that would
cut them into various lengths and sizes.

Each pit-prop was stacked according to it's length and dia-
meter. There were seventeen sizes in softwood and the same
number in hardwood.

I began work stacking at the sawmill, along with James
McNamara. We were kept pretty busy and in no time at all
one could raise a sweat. I remember my first Saturday stack-
ing at the mill in Rossagoale. When we stopped at one o'clock,
I threw myself on a pile of sawdust to take a breather. When
I rose again the outline of my body was left behind in sweat.

Work proceeded. Like weary old wasps whose nest had
been despoiled by a deluge of rain, yellow tractors crept and
crawled through high stacks of timber or grunted and growled
all day long in the depths of the wood. The pit-props were
stencil-numbered for removal to the waggons at the railway
station. Lorries lumbered along the narrow roads bearing great
loads of logs and whined in protest as they ascended a steep
incline.

But when the thinnings were processed and the systematic
felling of the entire forest commenced, it moved me to con-
sult with the Muses Nine and pen a poetic protest. It took the
title of *The Battle of Rossagoale* and the fact that a world
war was being waged may account for some of the imagery
used. Here is the poem:

In Rossagoale the trumpet blast
Of winter, roaring through the pines
Began the war; the trees held fast
Their strength entrenched in endless line

And though the winter's frosty fangs
Gnawed hard to nip their life away
The trees withstood the piercing pangs
And side by side withstood the fray.

Then springtide came with flowery feet
And winter hastened on the march
But low! the trees hemmed his retreat
With spear of spruce and lance of larch

Destroyer ducklings, row on row
Are feasting in the oats and wheat
But harking to the pheasant's crow
Rush out to join the Erne fleet

Above the water like a spear
A perch's coning fin is seen
But warship swans a-cruising near
Hail him, their friendly submarine

In Rossagoale the axes ring
And lordly trees in battle fall
Down by the lake the waters fling
Around the shivering shore a shawl

The sawmill sings a wicked song
A song of sin and blood and death
And trees that stood the storm for long
Shriek vengence in their dying breath

And back behind the buzzing saw
The lifeless trees rise stack on stack
The vicious teeth that nip and gnaw
Through woody sinews never slack

Around the road that runs the shore
The lumbering lorries ever roll
Their timber-laden engines roar
"Defeat and death to Rossagoale!"

Strange as it may seem now I was proud of that poem and made bold to enter it for a competition in the *Irish Weekly Independent,* the only publication in this country at the time that in any way encouraged climbers of Mount Parnassus. To my utter delight it won the current half-guinea prize and was published a fortnight later. At that time my weekly wages were twenty-two shillings and I had weathered nineteen summers. Could the pen be an easier way to make a living than the axe?

At that time I knew little of the fickleness of the Muses or the struggle it is to advance even one step further up the steep slopes of Parnassus. Miss Hilda O'Boyle, my former English teacher, was also very pleased and lent me *Wuthering Heights* to further my literary advancement.

However, it was not considered proper for a lumber jack to indulge in the reading of English classics during the dinner hour. I was reminded of this by a veritable hail of wooden chips showered on me from the tree stump near the Covered Well where Pat Gormley pointed picket posts. This did not deter me in the least, and when I refused to be intimidated they settled down again to their mid-day nap or to inanities about the scarcity of tea or the price of cattle, leaving me to roam the Yorkshire moors in the company of Cathy and Heath-cliff.

Tom Kane and Pat Gormley, God rest them both, were two of the old-timers on our team of timbermen, and veritable treasure-houses of stories and local lore. I can recall clearly a summer spent with these two heroes in the Hare Park, where we were sent to bark pit-props. This operation meant exactly what it said although one wag who worked in the wood insisted that yelping was a better word to describe the operation. In short the bark was shorn off the pit-props and logs, with the aid of a tool known in the trade as a barking iron, to prolong the life span of the timber.

The work was not hard and we were paid by the linear foot. Indeed it was relatively easy to make the week's wage, once we got used to the barking irons, and thereafter the few extra shillings could be picked up.

Tom had a wonderful story about a pedlar who plied his trade around the country when the old woodman was still at school. He went under the name of Giolla Rua and it was whispered that the same Giolla had the coaxelorum, a concoction that compelled all animate females imbibing it to follow him. And signs on him, hadn't he roughly seven wives at the one time! When a quarrel or a disputation arose in the tent that protected them from the elements, the Giolla would admonish them severely: "Agree ye divils ye", he used to say, "there's not that many of ye in it!"

This day, anyhow, he was peddling up the Toura country and sold a pair of blankets to a good-looking girl near Farrincassidy Cross. The girl was delighted with her bargain and, right enough, she had got it for a song, so she invited the Giolla to have tea and he consented. She brewed him a mug of good strong tea, the kind you could trot a mouse on if you know what I mean, and cut him three or four slices of home-

made bread all bright and goldened over with sweet country
butter. The Giolla did the morsel justice for in troth he had
just taken the *féar gortach* as he entered the mouth of the
lane leading to her house.

"Now", said he, as he reached her back the mug and
thanked her profusely, "maybe you'd have a wee trate on me.
Could you fetch us two tumblers, if you please?" He seemed
and affable sort of man so she brought the glasses. He took a
naggin bottle out of his inside coat pocket and carefully poured
the contents into the two tumblers in equal measure. "Good
health!" he toasted, "may you never want warm fleecy
blankets," but there was a glint in his eye that made her
swither. She put the glass to her lips, pretending to drink, and
moved down to the half-door. Out of the side of her eye she
watched him move to the fire, knuckle a knee on the hearthstone, and raise a coal to his pipe in the toes of the tongs. She
waited until the heat of the coal made him blink and then as
he hollowed his cheeks with the first smalk, she leant out and
emptied her glass into a cavity between the flags where a flock
of ducks were whottling.

The Giolla departed in high spirits. When he was going at
Slaters, some four miles away, he chanced to look round.
There, strung out in a straight row, their chassis swinging pen-
dulously from side to side, waddled the whole flock of ducks
and there was not a drake among them!

"You céilíed to Micky Flanagan's, Tom! Tell us about the
time he found the four-leafed shamrock." Pat coaxed him.

"Troth I did many's a time. I used to cross the Scolobin
in the boat to make my céilí. We had some rare nights in the
same house. I think maybe there was a drop of poteen sent
for the night we gathered to see the four-leafed trefoil. He
plucked it of a Saturday evening in a sheltery corner of the
field where a maiden mare dropped her first foal. A lot of
people think that the only merit of the four-leafed shamrock
is the protection it affords against witches and evil spells. The
great advantage of having one of them is, of course, that
you can understand the language of the birds of the air and
the beasts of the field. Do you know that, Pat Gormley?"

"O I knew that since I was the height of your knee, not breaking your discourse, Tom." Pat assured him.

"Well, anyhow, there were a right lock of us sitting round so we made a 'join' and sent away to Carmichael's for the poteen. When the drink arrived and every man got a jorum, tongues got a bit loose and some one made bold to ask Micky if he really had got a sprig of the lucky clover. 'Indeed I did', Micky told us, 'but I can't show it to you. That would destroy it's powers'. With that, the rooster on the henroost, between the dresser and the back door, roused himself, pecked a hen on the head and knocked her down to a lower perch, flapped his wings and crowed loudly. I can tell you we were frightened, drink and all.

"'What did the rooster say when he made all that fuss Micky?' Willie McCabe inquired, giving Micky that sly old look that was his wont. 'Well now', said Micky, as cute as hell, 'I'd rather not tell you, for it concerns one of our number.' 'Out with it, out with it!' we all shouted, 'there's none of us that thin-skinned.' 'Alright, since you want it you'll get it, but far be it from me to afront one of my céilíers. The rooster said if Daniel Dolan had done the same with his girl-friend she wouldn't have left him for any pock-marked policeman.' Daniel jumped to his feet and they tell me he never quit running till he was in Bonnahill. The rest of us céilied on until bedtime. When we rose to go, Micky conveyed us to the gable of the house, as is the custom, and, as we stood around studying the stars and watering the horses, the dogs of the seven townlands began to bark.

"'What oul' chat are them dogs at," Peter Duffy asked Micky. 'Shisht, man, and let me listen a wee while. They're all speaking together as you all can hear, but that big deep voice says he's from Derrincrannóg and he's telling the Tierygannon dogs over here that there's a donkey dead in Garvery and for them to hurry up or the Derrarona dogs will have him all ate!'"

Pat fell off the stack of pit-props with the laughing. When there were no foremen around and the quantity of timber we had stripped far exceeded our quota for the day, we relaxed and fell completely out of time. Stretched flat in the great wreaths of spruce branches that had been loped off the felled timber, kissed by the sun of a southern sky and fanned by a cool breeze that blew up from the Sandy Bay, we tarried in the timelessness of Tírnanóg and told our tales. I should like to think that I captured the mood in another flirtation with the Muses many years later. Here it is:

AXE-REST
To the knee of an oak we braced our backs
With foreheads sweaty and resin-matted
For space of an hour no man swung axe
But sprawled in the spruce and raved and chatted
And horny heifers were bought and sold
And women wooed for their dark-eyed glances
Till birdsong leaping in loops of gold
Ran wild with our hearts through céilí dances

O balm for the bruise of a cross-cut tooth
Or pimple prickled by pine-bark poison
O yearning forged in the fires of youth
And vision vaulting beyond horizon
And all life poised in a pain-pith ache
That splits the soul in a thousand splinters
For springs and summers are doomed to take
A tomb in the weary waste of winters.

Pat Gormley was a seasoned old campaigner in every sense of the word. He was a champion mower, a fine sawyer, an expert with an axe and a skillful if speedy thatcher. He had been hired as a spalpeen, or farm labourer, at an early age and the conditions under which he worked were grisly in the extreme. His attitude towards the fair sex was singularly cynical, but that he had once ended up in bed with a woman, he freely admitted. In fact the story of that adventure was one of his best. "It happened this way", he began. "James McGirr had me pestered to thatch the house up at the chapel and when he told me he had the straw drawn and the scollops made and ready, I headed away one morning at the screak of day, the way I'd have the back nearly thatched before the neighbours would rise out of their beds. I hadn't a notion there was anyone living in the old rickling for I thought all the McGirrs were stopping below in Lowryban. There was a ladder up on the roof of the house at the back when I arrived and I never bothered to take it down and test the rungs or a hate. I grabbed a sheaf of straw and a bundle of scollops and started my first spar. There was a lot of stappling to be done under the skew of the southern gable and I was up and down that ladder like a jack-in-the-box. Damn it, I must have bogged a whole stook of straw in the hole the blackbirds had made. In the latter end, I had her in fair old shape and lent out over the rigging to apply the finishing touch. With that the three rungs under me snapped, the rafters and roof caved in and I lit straddle-legged on Kate in the bed.

"You know Kate's form. No billhook or sickle I ever sharpened, and I'm a brave hand at the job, could clip a thorn hedge as clean as that tongue of hers, but when she started on the back trail and read me up for seven generations back, it was tight to thole it. I can hear the curses and scolds of her till this day. Divil mend her anyway. She may not have known I was coming to thatch but she lay up there like a churn adrying and I thatching and thumping on the roof above her till I made the forced landing. Still I suppose I'm the only man ever saw her in her shift."

Tom Kane shook with laughter. "Damn it, Pat, you should have married her", he ventured, "and she with a farm of land of her own and all." "Nawh, I shouldn't and I didn't. No man alive will ever say of Pat Gormley:

But the vows you made sure you went and broke them,
And married the lassie who had the land."

I started. Where had I heard those words before? I inquired off Pat if he had the rest of the song but he said not.

"Young fellow", he told me solemnly, "if there's a singer alive who has that song it'll be your own mother."

I went home somewhat excited and quoted the two lines to my mother. Yes, she had the song. It was called *The False Bride* and also *As I Roved Out*. She promised to sing it next time she'd be in voice.

It was the time of the long bright evenings coming into the mouth of the mowing. Meadow mane rippled with corn-crakes and scythe steel sang to whetstone. The air ached with the pain and joy of living. It was the time that turned my mother to songs of love and longing, and the two lines from *The False Bride* I had asked her about a fortnight before gently jerked her mind towards them.

She put aside the hoops that held the cloth, whereon her needle and thread had wrought the most exotic rosebuds, open flowers and intricate patterns, and wove with her voice arabesques of sound that bested the embroidery. She sang me for the first time that exquisitely beautiful song — *As I Roved Out* or *The False Bride:*

As— I roved out— on a bright May morn - ing
To view the mead - ows— and flow - ers— gay
Whom— should I spy— but my own true lov - er
As she— sat un - der— a will- ow tree.

I took off my hat and I did salute her
I did salute her courageously
When she turned around and the tears fell from her saying:
"False young man you have deluded me."

"For to delude you, how can that be my love
It's from your body I am quite free.
I'm as free from you as the child unborn is and
So are you too, dear Jane, from me."

"Three-diamond ring sure I own I gave you
Three-diamond ring to wear on your right hand."
"But the vows you made love, you went and broke them and
Married the lassie who had the land."

"If I married the lassie who had the land, my love,
It's that I'll rue till the day I die.
Where misfortune falls sure no one can shun it I
Was blindfolded I'll never deny."

Now at night when I go to my bed of slumber
The thoughts of my truelove run on my mind.
When I turn around to embrace my darling In-
stead of gold sure it's brass I find.

And I wish the queen would call home her armies
From the West Indies, America and Spain,
And every man to his wedded woman in
Hopes that you and I would meet again.

"Then there's *Craigie Hill,*" she'd say, "a song seldom heard these times."

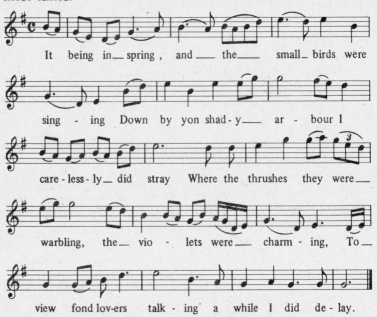

It being in— spring , and — the— small— birds were sing - ing Down by yon shad - y— ar - bour I care - less - ly— did stray Where the thrushes they were— warbling, the— vio - lets were— charm - ing, To— view fond lov-ers talk - ing a while I did de - lay.

She said: "My dear don't leave me for another season
Though fortune does be pleasing I'll go along with you.
I'll forsake friends and relations and quit this Irish nation
And to the bonnie Bann banks for ever I'll bid adieu."

He said: "My dear don't grieve me, or yet annoy my patience
You know I love you dearly, the more I'm going away.
I'm going to a foreign nation to purchase a plantation
To comfort us hereafter all in Americay.

"Then after a short while if fortune does be pleasing
'Twill cause them for to smile at our late going away.
We'll be happy as Queen Victorie all in her greatest glory
We'll be drinking wine and porter all in Americay.

"The landlords and their agents, the bailiffs and their beagles
The land of our forefathers we're forced for to give o'er.
Now we're sailing on the ocean for honour and promotion
And parting with our sweethearts, 'tis them we do adore.

"If you were on your bed lying and thinking on dying
The sight of the bonnie Bann banks your sorrow you'd give o'er,
Or if you were one hour down in yon shady bower
Pleasure would surround you, you'd think on death no more.

"Then fare you well sweet Craigie Hill where often times I have roved.
I never thought my childhood days I'd part you anymore.
Now we're sailing on the ocean for honour and promotion
And the bonnie boats are sailing 'way down by Doorin shore."

Another delightful song of hers, which she sang on that occasion but witheld from me for years, was a song of occupation and hailed from Stone Fiddle country along Lough Erne shore. It is called *The Wee Weaver:*

I am a wee wea-ver con-fined to my loom, My love she's as fair as the red rose in June. She is loved by all others and that does grieve me My heart's in the bo-som of love-ly Ma-ry.

As Mary and Willie roamed by yonder green bower
Where Mary and Willie spent many a happy hour
Where the thrush and the linnet do consort in chore
To sing the praises of Mary, round Lough Erne Shore.

As Mary and Willie roamed by yonder lough side
Said Willie to Mary "will you be my bride?"
So this couple got married and they'll roam no more,
They'll have pleasures and treasures round Lough Erne Shore.

Tom Mulhartagh lived near Tullaghawaine, that townland famed for milk-cows. It appears that it was the only spot the Glas Gaibhlinn grazed, on the few sorties she made across from Northwest Donegal for a good drink out of Lough Erne. It seems the Donegal loughs were on the small side to slake a thirst raised by a bellyful of bad poteen they gave her beyond on Tory Island. The old people will still tell you that, on her last visit, she nearly drank Lough Erne dry. Being a fairy cow, anywhere she grazed or dropped her dung was endowed with the richest and greenest grass to be found within the four shores of Ireland.

She had an inexhaustible supply of milk and it mattered not how much milk was drawn from the silken teats, the poor man's pail was always left behind. Little wonder that a cow with such a flow of milk should have a mighty thirst, even without the baleful Tory beverage to aggravate it.

But Tom Mulhartagh's concern was not with large and legendary cows. His time was taken up with that

> Leper of ditches, the clipper of thorns
> The wee brown cow, with the pair of leather horns.

In short he was an expert on hares. If your cows were not milking to capacity and they were in sound health, there could be only one reason. A witch-hare was at her nefarious work. Tom's muzzle-loader, with a silver sixpence substituted for lead shot, was the remedy. You see silver is the only metal can penetrate the hide of a witch-hare. Besides, Tom was a top marksman and he always aimed at the fleshy part of the hip or thigh.

When he winged one of them, as she perched on her hind legs and sucked a cow, he invariably raced her home, where he found her lying prone on the hearth, once more in the

form of an old woman and she bleeding profusely. The gable
window through which she had made her re-entry as a wounded
hare, he found open. He had always staunched the blood
with a cobweb he drew down from the scollop points, that
speared through the roof scraws, and then bound the limb
tightly with a bandage made from a bed-sheet. After such
medical treatment, it was easy to extract a solemn promise
from the unfortunate hag to give up witch-haring. Tom, on
his part, vowed never to disclose her identity, at least as long
as she lived. "It always works", he told us proudly. "It's a
holy and just terror, the number of hags I cured completely
of witch-haring!" None of us doubted Tom's word.

Mulhartagh was either in league with the fairies or else he
was a ventriloquist. Otherwise, how could he carry on con-
servations with the wee people, ensconeed somewhere up the
sooty chimney? When he addressed them, the answering
voices were always clear and melodious. We all heard them as
we sat around in the glow of the firelight. Could he have
been possessed of some special occult powers not fully
understood by himself? We shall never know.

He could also diagnose the disease known as "elf-shot",
quite common in the bovine kingdom at that time. However
he always had to send for Pat Lawn to aid him in effecting a
cure. The condition was quite serious and inevitably led to
death if these two gentlemen were not alerted. The disease
was contracted by a slight flesh wound from an elfin arrow
and the onset was attended by obvious pain, swelling of the
belly and loss of milk. Diagnosis was carried out by measur-
ing the cow with a prickly briar, the two ends of which had
been rooted in the ground. One root was held at the top of
the beast's nose and the briar was passed out between her
horns to whatever point down her backbone the length of the
briar reached. It was then moved again and another measure
taken to the tip of her tail and back via her udder, up her
belly and out between the forelegs and up the neck back to
the nose tip. She was then left for three days and again
measured and if she had increased in bulk she was elf-shot.
The treatment consisted of a mixture of molten silver and

brass which was poured into her right ear accompanied by the words, "shake it out, girl, shake it out, girl!" A quantity of the metal was retained to be buried at the stake. Then a red-hot coal was held on the tongs at the beast's nose, by the head-doctor himself, Pat Lawn, and in the course of a couple of hours the beast was restored to perfect health.

"No good sportsman would shoot a hare; it is for coursing only", we were often told, and surely Tom Mulhartagh could not be accused of bad sportsmanship. Yet he did not mind taking a pot at natural hares, as well as witch-hares, if the occasion demanded.

Maybe an expectant mother would get a longing for hare soup or a winter 'flu would hang too long on one of the hoary old heroes in those hills. If so, Tom was asked to procure the makings of the soup and he invariably obliged. This year he himself was the victim of the hang-over 'flu. The feast of Saint Brigid came and went and before he found, wasn't he on the threshold of Lent and still coughing and wheezing. He'd have to make his move soon or the hares would be out of season.

It was a dark, dreary day in the latter-end of February, with a black, bitter wind blowing from Russia that would bore holes in you. Tom let the cows out to drink at the river for he was too weak to draw water for them. As he came back to the shelter of the byre, he spied a big brown hare feeding in the meadow field below the black sally bushes. He slipped back to the house and reached up to the mantelpiece for the box that he kept his mould and bar of lead in and other odds and ends.

He rummaged about in the box and finally drew out his mould and bar of lead, as he thought. The daylight was fading rapidly so with the aid of a good fire he melted his shot and ran it through the moulds.

In next to no time he was back in the sally bushes, his gun primed, charged and ready for action.

The hare was crouched low on all fours, cropping away at the short grass.

Tom whistled softly and the animal raised itself on it's

hind legs and sniffed the air furtively. Mulhartagh put the
muzzle-loader to his shoulder and let go. The hare neither
fell nor staggered but bucklepped up the meadow and headed
for the heather beyond. Poor Tom was dumbfounded. Surely
this could not be yet another witch-hare. He was not in the
habit of missing and so he left aside the gun and hurried after
the retreating animal. Just above at a narrow gap in the sod
fence, made by the sheep breaking into the meadow, he came
on his quarry pulling tug-o'-war with another hare, their hindquarters stuck tightly together. He closed with them and captured both without much of a struggle. It was then he learned
the cause of their predicament. In this hurry and with the
failing light he had mistaken a bar of cobbler's wax for the
lead, so that it was wax balls that went into the gun. He had
found his mark alright and the beast had been plastered with
molten wax that only bonded as the hares brushed backsides
in the narrow gap. "Of course", Tom always added when telling this story, "in those days, cobbler's wax was cobbler's
wax!"

Which brings me to that lovely song of a remarkable white
hare that ran, not so many moons ago, on the turf banks of
Creggan:

THE CREGGAN WHITE HARE

In the lowlands of Creggan there lies a white hare;
She's as swift as a swallow that flies through the air.
You may travel this country and but there's none to compare
With the pride of low Creggan, the bonnie white hare.

One fine Sunday morning as you may suppose,
As the red golden sun o'er the green fields arose,
Barney Conway came round and so loud did declare
He says: "I'll put an end till your Creggan White Hare."

He searched through the lowlands and down through the glens
And among the green rushes where the white hare had dens
'Till at last coming home on a bog-bank so bare
From behind a white thistle out jumps the white hare.

He gave a great gulder and his dogs he slipped too
Across the green meadows a beautiful view
But the dogs soon came back which made poor Barney sigh
For he knew that the white hare had bid him goodbye.

We have some jolly sportsmen down here from Pomeroy,
Cookstown, Dungannon and also the Moy
With pedigree greyhounds they came from afar
And they travelled to Creggan in a fine motor-car.

'Twas down through the lowlands these huntsmen did go
To search for the white hare they tried high and low
'Till at last Barney Conway, as he came on its lair,
Shouted out to the sportsmen: "here lies the white hare."

They called in their greyhounds from off the green lea
And Barney and the huntsmen they jumped high with glee.
'Twas on the turf bank they all gathered around,
Seven men and nine dogs did the white hare surround.

No wonder the poor puss did tremble with fear
As she stood on her toes she would raise her big ear.
But she ris on her toes and with one gallant spring
Cleared over the greyhounds and broke through the ring.

The chase it went on 'twas a beautiful view,
As swift as the wind o'er the green valleys flew.
But these pedigree greyhounds they didn't go far.
They came back and went home in their fine motor-car.

So now to conclude and to finish my rhyme
I hope you'll excuse me for wasting your time.
If there's any amongst you in Carrickmore Fair
Drink a jolly good health to the Creggan White Hare.

Red Eddie Lawn lay away back in a maze of blackberry bramble on the head of Seanbhaile, his crown of copper curls as wild and wayward as the briars that sprouted around him.

"I got this one from Uncle Johnnie", he told me. "You mind him. He lived in Brookhill above." It was well I remembered his uncle Johnnie Monaghan, who had sung songs and told stories for Sam Hanna Bell's *It's A Brave Step* programmes in the early fifties. *The Colleen Deas* and *The Orangemens' Trousers I Bought In Belcoo* were his great favourites. Eddie looked out over Lough Erne and began in that quiet, effortless style of his:

I won-der what's keeping my true love to-night, I—
won-der what's keep-ing him out of my sight, O—
lit-tle he knows all the pain I en-dure Or he
would not— stay— from me this— night I am sure.

O love are you coming my pain to advance
Or, love, are you waiting for a far better chance
Or have you a sweetheart laid by you in store
Or are you coming for to tell me that you love me no more?

O love, I'm not coming your pain to advance
Or, love, do I wait for a far better chance
Or have I but a sweetheart laid by me in store
But I'm coming to tell you that I love you no more

I have gold in my pocket and love in my heart
But I can't love a maiden who has got two sweethearts
I love you just lightly like the dew on the thorn
That comes down in the evening and goes away in the morn

Green grass it grows bonnie, spring water runs clear
I weary, I weary, when I think of you, dear
You were my first and fond truelove, but it's now do I rue
The fonder I loved you the falser you grew

Come, all you young maidens, take a warning from me
Never build your nest on the top of a tree
The roots they will wither, and the branches decay
Like the false-hearted young man, they will soon fade away

Eddie had many other songs, mostly with a local flavour, but none of them can compare in beauty and poignancy with this magnificent love song. He is also a keen observer of nature and is familiar with the habits and haunts of the fish, the fowl and the furry friends of river, lake and forest.

"Patrick", he told me solemnly," if you want a pheasant or two in season, you'd be a fool to go out with a gun and start blarging at them. I leave out a small sheaf of oats round about Hallowe'en. Just enough to start them feeding, do you understand? Very soon they come along to pick the grains. Every day I bring a big sceilp of a sharp stone to the spot so that when the black frost comes there's a complete stone circle around the pheasants' feeding ground. The frost seals off their water supply and it is then I leave out around a pint of poteen in a heavy earth jar, the way they won't turn it over. As you know the poteen won't freeze. Pheasants getting their corn are in fine fighting fettle, but when they get a couple of jorums of the craythur itself there's no holding them. A fight breaks out and they knock out each others' brains out on the sharp edges of the stones. You can go along quietly in the morning and pick up the dead warriors and those of them that are still sleeping it off!

Eddie could direct you unerringly to the habitat of the last pine martens in Fermanagh but, being a sensible man and a great lover of that rare species, he would not. His novel knack of fowling put me in mind of a story told me once by an ex-RIC sergeant relating to the adventures of a young policeman, home on leave at Christmas, in the county of Mayo.

He was wild about fowling and his great ambition was to wing a wildgoose. To this end he set out, armed with a borrowed, double-barrelled shotgun. It was Saint Stephen's Day and a thick mist lay low on the hills, held down by a frosty rime that furred the eye-lashes.

He travelled all day, skirting mountain lakes and moorland marshes where the geese were wont to feed, but plume or feather he failed to find. Towards evening, when the dusk was drawing black brows down over the last gleed of God's good daylight, didn't he hear the honk of geese in the mist above him.

As he concealed himself in the whins and tensed himself for a shot, they broke through the fog, and half-mooned round to light on a little pond of a lough below him and quite near his home. They were well within range, so he put the fowling-piece to his shoulder, pulled left and pulled right.

It was then he heard an unmerciful yell and, looking over the sod fence he saw old Willie Shannon keel over at the face of his potato pit. Good God! Could the old man have been in his line of fire? And then he panicked. Throwing the gun from him, he ran the three miles to the crossroads pub in record time. Until that evening he didn't know the taste of drink, but the pint of whiskey he ordered was drained to the dregs and he still as sober as a judge, waiting for the local police to come and arrest him for murder, when old Willie Shannon burst in the bar door. His first reaction was to scream, for he thought it was the old fellow's ghost, but when Willie waxed forth in praise of the Almighty he was assured the old codger was alive and kicking. "O Glory be to God!" declared the old man, "If a miracle hashn't happened that I may be shtuck to the floor I'm shtanding on. I waishe lifting a bag of potatoes at the pit above barely an hour ago when theshe three geeshe flopped down out of the misht and made to light on the lough. From force of habit, I threw the shpade to my shoulder and took aim down the shaft. I had the three birds dead in my shights. 'Boys o boys', I longed, 'if you were only a gun!'

"With that the shpade went off with two thunderous bangs and I don't know if it waish the shudden shock or the fierce kick of the shpade — for I wasn't holding her tightly — that shtretched me on the broad of my back for a quarter of an hour. When I came to again, there were my three geeshe floating in among the bullreeds, dead ash dodosh. Any of you who don't believe what I shay can come back with me to the houshe and shee for himself. The three fine birdsh are hanging there on the harnessh peg in the kitchen."

The young policeman ran over to the old hero and hugged him heartily. He was drunk with relief and delight that he hadn't taken a life and bought a bumper of whiskey for Willie.

The old man lived for another seven years. During that space of time the fame of the magic spade spread far and wide, away out over the Ox Mountains and into Coleman country around Ballymote. Pious men and superstitious ones made pilgrimages to see the weapon and gazed upon it with awe and wonder. Willie proudly displayed it to all comers, but was careful never to point it at anyone. "With sphades you can never be sure", he told them, "They haven't got shafety catches, you shee!"

The young policeman, for his part, kept the secret until after Willie's death. He hated to tell him the true story and thereby shatter a wonderful legend.

18. MY UNCLE MICHAEL
AND THE CROSS CEILI HOUSE

The war was over and soldiers were returning from front line positions, prison camps and prisons. It was only natural I suppose that, with the goodwill generated at the time, young mens' hearts should turn to love and lovesongs. To the old-timers, who were the song carriers of the people and who passed on a priceless heritage, it never ceased to be a source of wonder and delight that such interest was taken in their offerings.

My Uncle Michael, or Mick as he was mostly called, may his lodging be bright in the halls of heaven, returned to Ireland in nineteen hundred and forty eight. He was a shoemaker and set up in the townland of Tunnynoran, after thirty years of exile in Glasgow. He had never lost touch with the old tradition and played both melodeon and fiddle reasonably well. He also sang and had a rich store of humorous songs. Perhaps his best known song is *The Rollicking Boys around Tandragee,* in which a good-homoured swipe is made at quite a few sacred cows. *(Air: The Bunch of Green Rushes that Grew on the Brim [double jig].).*

Good luck to all here now, barring the cat
That sits in the corner there smelling a rat
O wheesht your philandering girls and behave
And saving your presence, I'll chant you a stave
I come from the land where the pritties grow big
And the boys neat and handy can swirl in a jig
And the girls they would charm your heart for to see
Those darling colleens around Tandragee.

Chorus

So here's to the boys who are happy and gay
Singing and dancing and tearing away
Rollicksome, frollicsome, frisky and free
We're the rollicking boys around Tandragee.

No doubt you have heard of Killarney I'm sure
And sweet Innishowen for a drop of the pure
Dublin's the place for the strawberry beds
And Donnybrook Fair for the cracking of heads
Have you e'er seen an Irishman dancing palltog
How he faces his partner and turns up his brog
He shakes at the buckle and bends at the knee
They're wonderful dancers in Tandragee.

Chorus

Now the oul' jaunting-car is an elegant joult
And Derry's the place that is famed for a hoult
Among the green bushes that grow in Tyrone
And the County Fermanagh for muscle and bone
But for feasting and dancing and fun at the fair
Sure there's no one can match with the Rakes of Kildare
Green Erin my country's the gem of the sea
But the gem of oul' Ireland is Tandragee

Chorus

O where is the man, either Christian or Turk
Could equal the boul' Robert Emmet or Burke
Or where is the lawyer can speak up like Dan
The divil another, bad luck to the wan
And where is the singer can sing like Tom Moore
Whose melodies charm all dull care from our dure
But we'll beat them all yet boys, and that you will see
For we're raring fine fellows round Tandragee.

Chorus

"That", he maintained, "is the satire to slay all stage-Irishmen!" And who am I to disagree? Another great favourite with Uncle Mick was *The Cetch in the Creel,* a song that, because of the amorous implications it contained, he was loathe to sing in the presence of the fair sex.

As I went down through Newry Town some fresh fish for to buy
Whom did I spy but a pretty fair maid and on her I cast the glad eye

Courant

With my roor riha foldi dee thee da
Roor riha foldol the dee

How do I get to your chamber love, how do I get to your bed?
My father keeps the door locked, and the keys lie under his head

Courant

Get a ladder newly made, of forty steps and three
And you come up to the chimney-top and come down in a creel
   to me.

Courant

No peace or rest could the old woman get with dreams running
      through her head
"I'll lay my life," said the gay old wife, "there's a boy in our
      daughter's bed."

Courant

Up the stairs the old man crept and into the room did steal
Silence lay where the damsel slept and he never twigged the creel

Courant

My curse upon you father, what brought you up so soon
To put me through my evening prayers and I just lying down

Courant

He went back to his gay old wife, he went back to she
She has a prayer-book in her hands, and she's praying for you and
      me.

Courant

No peace or rest could the old hag get, till she would arise and see
She came on the stumbling block and into the creel went she

Courant

The lad being on the chimney-top he gave the creel a hawl
Broke three ribs in the old woman's side and her arse came against
      the wall

Courant

On other occasions Mick would sing *The Twins* or *The One Thing and the Other*.

At the age of twenty one I was in the prime of life
My parents often told me to go and choose a wife
To go and choose a wife I knew little about the bother
At the same time I was thinking of the one thing and the other

Musha whacka rowdee dow now
Right fol the daddy
Musha whack a row de dow now
Right fol the dee

I went to a wee girl that I for some time knew
To tell her what my parents were advising me to do
What's your errant, cried the sister, what's your errant, cried the
        mother
And to cut the story short says I it's the one thing or the other.

Musha whacka rowdee dow now . . .
Now we have got married, we lead a happy life
I'm her loving husband, and she's my darling wife
We live in peace and unity, right well content together
In our daily occupation with the one thing and the other

Musha . . .
A year passed away and we never had a care
Now the people say that we're going to have an heir
It's a son cries the sister, it's a daughter cries the mother
And to cut the story short says I it's the one thing or the other

Musha . . .

Twas on a Sunday morning just as my story runs
Twas on a Sunday morning when first I heard the twins
It was on a Monday morning my grief I couldn't smother
As I listened to the squalling of the one thing and the other

Musha . . .

Even his songs of the Land War and landlordism, with all
it's attendant evils, had a spark of humour in them. For
example, listen to this little ditty describing the love and
affection in which bailiffs were held in those stirring days.

THE DEVIL AND BAILIFF MCGLYNN
One fine Sunday evening last summer, I was walking in Condae na
    Mí
When a pair of quare boyos cologing, before me I happened to see
To know what these boyos were up to, a trifle I hastened my walk
And in troth I soon learned their profession, when I came within
    range of their talk.
Now one of those boys was the Devil, the other was Bailiff McGlynn
The one was as black as the other, and both were as ugly as sin.
Said the oul' boy: "You know I'm the Devil and you are a bailiff I
    see."
"Is it the Devil himself sure that's in it, well that beats the Devil,"
    says he.

Close by at a patch of potatoes, a bonive was striving to dig
When a woman ran out and she shouted: "May the Devil take you
    for a pig!"
Said the bailiff: "now that's a fine offer, why not the the bonive?
    said he
"It's only her lips that have said it, and that's not sufficient for me."

A garsún ran out of a cottage and off with him over the field
"May the Devil take you!" said his mother, and she rattled a stone
    off his heels.
Said the bailiff: "now that 's a fine offer, why not take the garsún?
    says he.
"It was only her lips that have wished it, and that's not sufficient for
    me."

A young lad looked up from his playing, and off to his mother he
    sped.
"O, mother" says he, "there's the bailiff," and she clasped her two
    hands and she said:
"May the Devil take that ugly bailiff!" Said the oul' lad "Bedad,
    that'll do.
Twas straight from her heart that came surely, so Bailiff McGlynn I'll
    take you."

When Uncle Mick spat out the mouthful of tacks with which cobblers and shoemakers are wont to clutter that area between tongue and palate, he could declaim a love-song with any other swain who fell victim to Cupid's bow. He revelled in the range and drama of a song like *When A Man's in love He Feels No Cold,* and indeed he was the first man or woman I ever heard sing it.

When a man's in love, he feels no cold Like me not long a-go, As a he-ro bold to see my girl I ploughed through frost and snow The moon she gent-ly shed her light A-long my drear-y way, Un-til I came to that sweet spot, Where all my treasure lay.

I knocked at my love's window saying
My dear are you within
And softly she undid the latch
And shyly I slipped in
Her hand was soft, her breath was sweet
Her tongue did gently glide
I stole a kiss; it was no miss
And I asked her to be my bride

Take me to your chamber love
O take me to your bed
Take me to your chamber love
To rest my weary head
To take you to my chamber love
My parents they won't agree
So sit you down by yon bright fire
And I'll sit close to thee

Many a night I courted you
Against your father's will
You never once said you'd be my bride
So now my love sit still
To-night I have to cross the sea
To afar Columbia's shore
And you will never never see
Your youthful lover more.

Many a cold and stormy night
I came to visit you
When tossed about by cold wintry winds
Or wet by the morning dew
Tonight our courtship's at a close
Between my love and me
So fare thee well my favourite girl
A long farewell to thee

Are you going to leave me here?
O pray what can I do
I'll break through every bond of love
And go along with you
Perhaps my parents may forget
But surely they'll forgive
For from this moment I'm content
Along with you to live
So with a kiss the ring was closed
And the wedding it's going on
From courtship's cares these two are freed
These two are joined as one
So with a kiss the ring was closed
And the wedding it's going on
From courtship's cares they are released
They now are joined in one.

By far his best love song was the one he learned from Willie Meehan, or Billy's Willie as he was commonly called, who lived in the Far End of the townland of Tamur. It is called *Adieu Lovely Nancy.*

A - dieu Love - ly Nan - cy— for now I must leave you To the far - off West In - dies I'm bound for to — steer, But let my long jour - ney be of no trou - ble to you, My dear I'll come back in the course of a year.

Talk not of leaving me here, lovely Jemmy
Talk not of leaving me here on the shore
You know very well your long journey will grieve me
As you sail the wild ocean, where the loud billows roar

I'll cut off my ringlets all curly and yellow
And dress in the clothes of a young cabin boy
And when we are out on the dark rolling ocean
I will always be near you, my pride and my joy

Your lily white hands could not handle the cables
Your lily white feet to the top-mast won't go
Nor the cold winter storms you could not endure them
Stay at home Lovely Nancy where the wild winds won't blow

As Jemmy set sailing, lovely Nancy stood wailing
The tears from her eyes in great torrents did flow
As she stood on the beach sure her hands she kept ringing
Crying och! and alas! will I e'er see you more?

. As Jemmy was walking on the quays of Philadelphia
The thoughts of his true love they filled him with pride
Crying Nancy, lovely Nancy, if I had you here love
How happy I'd be for to make you my bride.

Jemmy wrote a letter to his own love Nancy
Saying if you do prove constant sure I will prove true
But Nancy was on deathbed and could not recover
The day that he left her forever he'd rue

Come all you young maidens a warning take by me
And don't trust a sailor or one of his kind
For first they will court you and then they'll deceive you
Their love it is tempestuous like the wavering wind.

Mick's of the Cross was a great céili-ing house. Master
O'Shea, Paul and Willie McCabe and Willie Aiken all called
in for a crack with the cobbler. Occasionally the big fiddler,
Phillip Breen, dropped in to swop a tune with him. One night
I called at the Cross and found the ramblers in full session.
It was a rich experience. To compound the performance, I
went away and wrote the poem, *The Man of Songs.* Here it is:

> "That day I scored the winning goal",
> The cobbler said, and seized the tongs
> He spat upon the half-burnt coal
> "A stranger boys, The Man of Songs!"
>
> He stooped beneath the lintel low
> A troubadour from legend lands
> And settling in the greeshagh glow
> Round blackthorn hasped a harper's hands
>
> The mountain marrow braced his bone
> Hard granite set in monarch mould
> His tongue untethered silver tone
> Of sweetest sound, well veined with gold
>
> An urchin from the shadows sprang
> And straddle-legged on an upturned creel
> He lilted loud: the rafters rang
> With riot of a rousing reel

The fiddle drew a long bent bow
And eager dancers couldn't wait
As fast they railied heel and toe
And flaked it out to Bonnie Kate

From flagstones faster fly the splanks
All fiddle-frenzied fat they flail
A sudden wheel to face the ranks
Their hobnails bring a handclap hail

"And now we'll have the Man of Songs"
The cobbler said, and silence fell
As if the love the lone heart longs
For, cast before it's binding spells

And music bounded in the breeze
By dark trout-throw and salmon-leap
Where shepherd pined and pressed his cheese
And moorcocks cackled in their sleep

He sang a song the mountains sing
When mating thunders in the blood
And torrent-torn temples fling
From high the fury of the flood

The last line spoken and the speed
Of lightening swept us from the peaks
Like Oisin from the famed White Steed
For spirit sings but mortal speaks

And as the cobbler raked the fire
And held once more the flat-toed tongs
He sought the Land of Heart's Desire
And lingered with the Man of Songs

God rest my father, he was a quiet man who used his words sparingly. Nevertheless, when in storytelling company he could turn a tale with the best of them. One night John Lawn was in making his céili and who should chance to come our way only Big Pat O'Connor and Ned Noble. There was the makings of a mighty night's crack in that kind of company.

John Lawn should have been an architect for he had the gift of reducing very large masses of land to his own tiny scale as the following story will illustrate.

"There was this Mulleek man who met a Garrison man one day walking up Americay street. "Damn it, John Francis", he says, "it must be going to rain for the wind's from Garrison."

He then went on to tell of the night himself and James McSherry were sent to Attie Duncan's for the poteen, when a join had been made in a house in the Tully where they were attending a dance. Some time before, Attie, who was a champion fighter in his own parts, had picked a quarrel in the Harvest Fair of Ballyshanny with Big John Lawn. Big John gave Attie a sevendable thrashing and Attie, on his part, had a long memory and a most unforgiving nature.

Consequently, when the men with the Mulleek accents beat on his door he was beside himself with glee. As he undid the bars and bolts on his kitchen door, he shouted again: "Who have I in it?" and they shouted back, "James McSherry and John Lawn." "Ha! Ha! John Lawn did you say, you're welcome here, John Lawn!"

He opened the door and peered out at them over the frame of an old hurricane lamp that provided the only light in the Duncan household when the sun went down.

"Come on in, John Lawn and James McSherry." They did as they were told and were amazed when Attie bolted and barred the door when he got them inside. He never bothered to tighten the leather whangs in his heavy boots nor to tidy down the breeches that still gathered in wrinkles around his knees exposing the flannel long-johns he wore inside them.

"I always heard it said, that if a man had the patience to wait long enough, his quarry would walk into the house to him," and he reached for a vicious looking reaping-hook that hung on the roof couple and began honing it. The two men were frightened out of their wits, and waited with indrawn breath for the next move.

"John Lawn", inquired Attie, "are you as good a man this night as you were two years ago in the Harvest Fair? Only this time I'll be armed. If you overcome me and this hook then you are the champion, but if I win I will cut off your head and keep it as a spoil of victory. McSherry here can bring back the body to Mulleek for burial. Do you agree to these terms?"

It took the two men half the night explaining to Attie that it was a case of mistaken identity and that the man with whom he duelled in the Harvest Fair was Big John Lawn, a giant of a man and not the lightly built Red John Lawn who now stood on his floor. In the heel of the hunt they convinced him and, taking their money, he gave them a jar of poteen.

However, when they arrived back in the Tully, with their lives and the supply of shiskey, there was no one to drink it. All the dancers had gone home and were fast asleep in their beds. So the two boys enjoyed themselves as long as the liquor lasted.

Ned Noble could be held on no ground. "I mind the time I was over in the cancer hospital in Manchester getting the spot cut off my lip," he began. "In them times they were not that well up in science and indeed it's many's the consultation they held with myself when their experts were clane bate.

"This day, anyway, weren't they operating on a man and they had his stomach out on the table scraping it when the bell rang for dinner-time. Away my bullie surgeons went and forgot to close and lock the operating theatre door.

"There was this big buck cat that kept us awake half the

night chasing and catterwailing with she-cats. He was very fond of tit-bits and didn't he steal into the theatre and ate the poor man's stomach. When the doctors came back at two o'clock and found the stomach gone, they were in a bit of a quandary. They sent for me. 'What would you suggest, Paddy?' — they always called me Paddy.

"'Well now boys,' I told them, 'I'm no surgeon but the sensible thing to do would be to go round to the slaughter-house and get the stomach of a young heifer or bullock and stick it into him. If you do so, it's my candid opinion the old worn-out one you spent all morning scraping at will never be missed.' Away goes the head surgeon and picks a nice tender young stomach, comes back and grafts it into the patient.

"All went well until he was able to take food again. The put him on milk foods first and eventually he got beef and broth and whatever was going. No matter how much food he ate the pangs of hunger never left him.

"It's a holy sight surely, with all their learning and the number of men and women they had knifed, that they had to come again to Ned for a solution. 'Well now', I told them, 'but I could be wrong, I don't think you are giving him the right diet.' There was a boyo out in the grounds with a lawn-mower, cutting away for all he was worth.

"'Now', says I, 'wouldn't it be a good thing if some of you men went out and brought him in an armful of grass to see if he'd be satisfied'. Arah man! the armful of grass was not at his head until he was munching away with great relish and he didn't leave a cuinneog of the grass!

"When I left the hospital he was lying there in the bed chewing his cud contentedly. Can you bate that?''

It was then my father asked Big Pat O'Connor to recite *The Old Hag's Rhyme.* Here it is:

Ere last night, about three weeks ago, I received a letter telling me of an old hag's death. I was so over-joyed at the sad news that every tear that fell from the nose of my belly split fifteen fathoms of turf and set a mill agoing.

I put my two shin bones in my pocket and my head under my arm, and away goes I, sitting down every minute, till I met John

Jarvis, a hackney coachman, driving nineteen dead jack-asses in an
empty steam coach heavily laden with seventy-seven grandeer buck
magpie and seventy-seven rounds of buck stirabout, which was to
appear at the Battle of Sebastapool.

I asked him where the old hag lived, and he said "On a high hill in
a low valley, where the wind never blew, nor the cock never crew,
behind up and down street where the wind never blew, nor the cock
never crew, behind up and down street where a mad dog bit a hatchet
and pigs wrestled for stirabout."

I marched on till I came to the Curragh of Kildare where I saw a
man run away with a stack of chimneys on his back. There were
twelve little boys and thirty-six little girls palying hide-and-go-seek
round a hayrick built of stones. There I saw a dog barking at a pock-
marked cat that was knitting a pair of stocking and dying with the
chincough.

I pushed on till I came to a wall that was no higher than a cabbage
stalk and no longer than from Patrick's Day to New York. There was
an old woman taking a drink out of the River Liffey. I pushed her in
and she was immediately burned alive in a blaze of cold water and
drownded in a shower of feathers.

I then fell severely ill with a holic-colic in my big toe, a toothace
in my shin bone and a headache in the back of my bladder. I was
sent to the Rock Hospital where I took a fit of laughing for thirteen
days and twenty-two nights. I was ordered a physic of thirteen pints
of eels' beastings, seven ounces of frogs' butter and some cock-
roaches' kidneys. All these were boiled up in a large, iron, wooden,
leather pot.

I then threw up lap-dogs, slap-dogs, water dogs and terriers.

At the time there was a great battle raging in the ocean of green
pays. The general was severely wounded. A bullet struck him in the
stomach and knocked his appetite asunder.

The names of the officers were: Annie Hib, Gilster and Gig, Harry
McAlly, John McAlly, Peg o' the Rump, Hop off the Bench, Badly
Mad, Bad Pay Run Away and Stand Still.

Pat's Old Hag drew great applause from the story-tellers
and, to put the head-sheaf on a night's story-telling, my father
spun the yarn of Andy Morrow.

Andy Morrow was not the full shilling. He lived out the
Glenelly Road between Pettigo and Kesh and ran messages
for his mother and the neighbours. His mother was having a

meitheal of men to put in her potatoes and sent Andy off to
Kesh for some liver and kidney to make them a tasty meal.
The only way Andy could remember the message he was sent
for was by crying it out as he went along.

As he ran along the country road he kept shouting at the
loud of his head: "Lights and livers come up! lights and livers
come up!"

He soon came to a spot on the roadside where a man lay
vomiting up his heart, for he had only started to drink and
this was his first encounter with that doughty old warrior,
the morning after the night before, and he had failed in his
search for a hair out of the dog that bit him.

He marshalled up all his strength and seized Andy by the
throat and threatened to trottle him if he didn't change his
tune to: "May they never come up! may they never come up!"

He hadn't gone too far until four stout men planting potatoes in a field near the road harkened to his cry. They rushed
out and laid hands on him heavily. When they had pounded
him to their satisfaction, they agreed to release him if he
changed his cry and in future said: "Where there goes one
down, may there come two up! Where there goes one down,
may there come two up!"

He went without heed or hinder until he was passing a grave-
yard where the remains of a decent man were being interred.
The mourners were scandalised at the strange prayer a fellow
Christian was uttering and taking him civilly aside they im-
plored him to change his prayer to: "May he rest in peace!
May he rest in peace!"

The road led past a moist, mossy part of the country, where
there were two large bullock stirks bogged to the belly in a
deep quagmire. Five stout men had worked strong tethers
under the hindquarters and forelegs of one bullock and as
Andy approached, they heaved him out on dry land. The
cry, "May he rest in peace." incensed them. One of their
number, a giant of a man, approached Andy, seized him by
the back of the neck and the seat of the trousers and threatened to throw him into the hole out of which the bullock
was rescued unless he changed his slogan to: "There's one out

and I hope the other will soon be out!" Andy was glad to escape with his life and promptly switched to: "There's one out and I hope the other will soon be out! There's one out and I hope the other will soon be out!"

Andy went airily on his way, shouting his new slogan: "There's one out and I hope the other will soon be out! There's one out and I hope the other will soon be out!"

All fared well until he came as far as a one-eyed fiddler, sawing away as he sat on a window-stool outside the forge at the cross-roads.

"There's one out and I hope the other will soon be out!" chanted Andy in his high-pitched voice, as he passed by. The poor fiddler went clean a shaughran in *The Swallow's Tail*. Seizing the fiddle by the neck, he brought it down hard on Andy's head, shattering it into smithereens.

"How dare you! how dare you!" he screeched at Andy. "What kind of a brute baste of a man are you at all? You should be praying: "I wish for more light! I wish for more light!"

Andy changed his tune for the last time and entered Kesh shouting: "I wish for more light! I wish for more light!"

The police barrack was on fire and so Andy was arrested and charged with attempting to cause a public mischief.

If you go down to our street inquire at number nine,
And you may pass one and you may pass two, but the
red haired one is mine,
With the rooria, fal da do ada, rooria she's a gay oul'hag.

Where the brae-face blazed with whin blossom under the shafts of a heeled-up spring-cart, I found the singer. He was hammering away at a large tin measure, called a pouchel, and was in high spirits.

"You make bigger measures than that", I teased him. "Any of them running a heat for Easter?"

"Go along", he reproved me, "I'm none of your still tinkers. Wouldn't I look well trotting away to the Bishop with my wee story, in place of the quiet chat I have once a year with the beardy Friar from Ards and he passing the caravan." At that time poteen-making, or any deed or action closely associated with the nefarious trade, was a reserved sin in the Diocese of Raphoe, and indeed in Clogher too.

The piebald was stamping fretfully beyond at a holly bush where he was tethered. I glanced in that direction and the tinker looked up for the first time.

"How much will you take and drive me to Rathmullan?" I asked him jocosely.

"Troth and I'll drive you for nothing if the harness fits you", he gave me back, "but first I must be given time to finish the song."

"Go ahead", I told him, "the day is long."

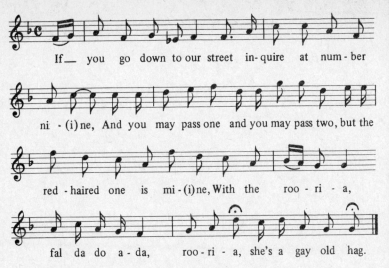

If— you go down to our street in-quire at num-ber ni-(i)ne, And you may pass one and you may pass two, but the red-haired one is mi-(i)ne, With the roo-ri-a, fal da do a-da, roo-ri-a, she's a gay old hag.

I sat her down on a bed of down, I sat her down right aisy
Three kisses then I stole from her and the last one drove her crazy
With the rooria, fol da do ada, rooria she's a gay oul' hag.

Oh I have money in my purse and money in my pocket
And if I have I'm telling you from the Newross girl I got it
With the rooria, fol da do ada, rooria she's a gay oul' hag.
Oh, I have a wife and a darlin' little wife, and I vow I'll not forsake
her
With a rooria, fol da do ada, rooria she's a gay oul' hag.

Paddy Doran continued with his very rare version of *Blackwater Side* and the sun shone down on us from a cloudless sky. I clean forgot I had been sent by the Town Clerk to ask the strange travelling man to leave Glencar, as it was a prohibited area for camping.

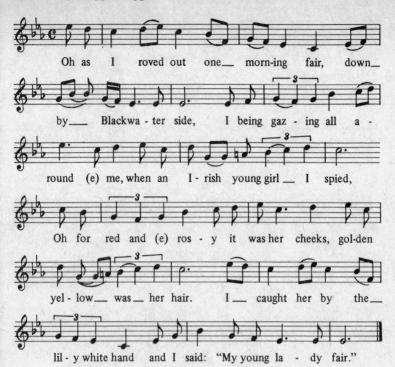

Oh as I roved out one____ morn-ing fair, down____
by____ Blackwa - ter side, I being gaz - ing all a -
round (e) me, when an I - rish young girl ___ I spied,
Oh for red and (e) ros - y it was her cheeks, gol-den
yel - low ____ was ___ her hair. I ___ caught her by the ___
lil - y white hand and I said: "My young la - dy fair."

There be many's a good man's daughter
going around from town to town
There be many's a good man's daughter
with her hair all hanging adown

They be rocking their cradles the whole day long
Singing loola and loola lo
Was there ever a poor misfortunate girl
was as easily led as you"

"That wasn't the promise you made to me
Down by Blackwater Side
That wasn't the promise you made to me,
When you asked me to be your bride
That wasn't the promise you made to me
When you swore to be loyal and true"
"When the fishes fly and the seas run dry,
I'll return and I'll marry you"

With a man like that to keep her company, it does not seem that Paddy's wife will ever be as desolate as the Cailleach Béara. His version of *The Raggle Taggle Gipsies* is a garbled one, but what it lacks in polish is more than made up for in raciness. Here it is and you can judge for yourself.

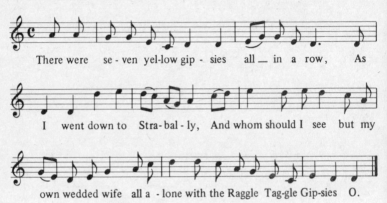

There were se-ven yel-low gip - sies all — in a row, As
I went down to Stra- bal - ly, And whom should I see but my
own wedded wife all a - lone with the Raggle Tag-gle Gip-sies O.

Come saddle for me, my pretty fair maid,
Saddle for me my pony O
For I wouldn't give a kiss off a gipsy lassie'd lips
For all oul' Squire Cash's money O.

Last night I lay on a cold barn floor
With seven yellow gipsies to annoy me O
But tonight I will lie on my own feather bed
With my own yellow gipsy all beside me O.

I had heard tell that he sang a fine version of *Edward,* but it took much coaxing before he sang that beautiful and dramatic ballad. Still, it was worth waiting for. Here it is as Paddy declaimed it on that magic morning, a quarter of a century ago. The voice was mellowing in the spring sunshine and the only distraction was the tiny pop of an early rippened whin pod.

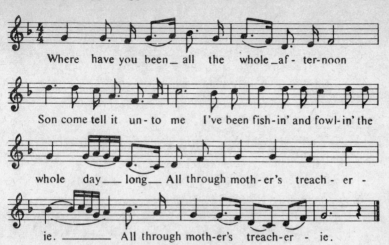

Where have you been— all the whole —af - ter-noon

Son come tell it un - to me I've been fish-in' and fowl-in' the

whole day—— long— All through moth-er's treach - er -

ie. ———— All through moth-er's treach-er - ie.

"What put the blood on your right shoulder?
        son come tell it unto me."
"Twas the killing of a hare that I killed today,
        that I killed most manfulliee,
        that I killed most manfulliee."

"The blood of the hare it could never be so red,
        son come tell it unto me."
"Twas the killing of a boy that I killed today,
        that I killed most manfulliee,
        that I killed most manfulliee."

"What came between yourself and the boy?
        son come tell it unto me."
"It was mostly the cutting of a rod,
        that would never come a tree, tree,
        that would never come a tree."

"What are you going to do when your Daddy finds you out?
        son come tell it unto me."
"I will put my foot on board of a ship
        and sail to a far-off countriee,
        and sail to a far-off counteriee."

"What are you going to do with your lovely young wife?
        son come tell it unto me."
"She can put her foot on board of a ship,
        and sail there after me-e,
        and sail there after me."

"What are you going to do with your two fine young babes?
    son come tell it unto me."
"I'll give one to my father and the other to my mother
    for to bear them companie-e,
    for to keep them companie."

"What are you going to do with your two fine race-horses?
    son come tell it unto me."
"I will take the bridles off their heads,
    for they'll race no more for me-e,
    they will race no more for me."

"What are you going to do with your two fine greyhounds?
    son come tell it unto me."
"I will take the leads all off their necks,
    for they'll run no more for me-e,
    they'll run no more for me."

"What are you going to do with your houses and your lands?
    son come tell it unto me."
"I will lay them bare to the birds of the air
    for there's no more welcome there for me-e,
    for there's no more welcome there for me."

"What will you do in the winter of your life?
    son come tell it unto me."
"Like a saggin on the lough I'll bend with the wind
    and I'll hope for God's mercie-e
    and I'll hope for God's mercie."

I bade farewell to Paddy Doran and, compounding my encounter with him and my only visit to Puck Fair in the great and glorious Kingdom of Kerry, I composed my own song about the Travelling People, *The Royal Visit*. Here it is:

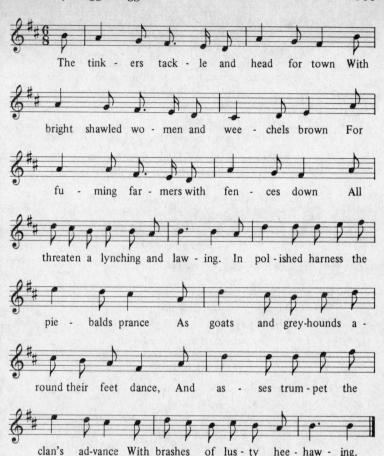

The tink - ers tack - le and head for town With
bright shawled wo - men and wee - chels brown For
fu - ming far - mers with fen - ces down All
threaten a lynching and law - ing. In pol - ished harness the
pie - balds prance As goats and grey-hounds a -
round their feet dance, And as - ses trum - pet the
clan's ad-vance With brashes of lus - ty hee - haw - ing.

They throng the side-walks and fill the fair
Great black-eyed boyos with horny hair
And not a cantman will cry his ware
As long as the tinkermen tarry
And bashful bachelors glimpse with glee
A curving bosom, an ankle or knee
And drunken drovers they all shout "wheeh!
No wonder these hammermen marry!"

Down gaping gullets the porter pours
And bowrans beat at the bar back-doors
Soon fists are flaying, a farmer roars:
"O why did you sell oul' Killarney?"
A strolling songster with voice as pure
As mountain stream on a heathery moor
Sings out *The Valley of Knockanure*
"My life on you, balladman Barney!"

A lissome lassie with eyes like sloes
To pub or alehouse she seldom goes
But o'er the threshold her laughter throws
To moider old men in their whiskey
A peeler spies her, a hard old crust,
His body stiffens with fierce stun of lust
He craves to plunder, and try he must
Though mating with her might be risky

He ventures nearer and vets her well
Of tinker women she is the belle
The quiet sort that would never tell
Her eyes to the archway she raises.
Well chizelled features, a bit too chaste
A ripe, round breast and a willowy waist
The hound within him is howling "haste,
Let caution and stealth go to blazes!"

The peeler pounces; no scream or call
He drags his prey to a stable stall
A panther springs from the darkened wall
He drops like an ox for the slaughter
A drink of teeth and a broken jaw
Is just reward for this limb of the law
Who dared his baton to ever draw
In taming the tinker king's daughter.

The dark man straightens with throaty snarls
And kicks the copper round empty barrels
Above, beyond them, a boglark carols
The clock in the Square's striking seven
The old king gathers the leather reins
The wild blood bucking in Romany veins
He heads again for the hills and plains
His castle the high dome of heaven.

In the whole corpus of traditional song couched in the borrowed Béarla, there are none to compare with the high-minded effusions of our hedge-school-master poets. These songs are readily recognisable by the plentitude of classical allusions they contain and by the adaptation of the Gaelic assonantal rhyme, used extensively by the Gaelic Aisling poets of the eighteenth century.

When the classes dispersed and the master roamed, with the great god Pan down in the reeds by the river, then surely it was that his mind took fire and he wrote such a song as *Lough Erne Shore.*

One morn-ing as I went a fowl-ing Bright Phoebus a-dorned the plain 'Twas down by the shores of Lough Erne I met with this won-der-ful dame Her voice was so sweet and so pleas-ing These beaut-i-ful notes she did sing The inn-o-cent fowl of the for-est their love un-to her they did bring.

115

It being the first time I saw her, my heart it did lep with surprise
I thought that she could be no mortal, but an angel who fell from
      the skies
Her hair it resembled gold tresses, her skin was as white as the snow
And her cheeks were as red as the roses that bloom around Lough
      Erne Shore.

When I found that my love was eloping these words unto her I did
      say
O take me to your habitation, for Cupid has led me astray.
For ever I'll keep the commandments, they say that it is the best
      plan
Fair maids who do yeild to men's pleasure, the Scripture does say
      they are wrong

O Mary don't accuse me of weakness, for treachery I do disown
I'll make you a lady of honour, if with me this night you'll come
      home
O had I the Lamp of Great Aladdin, his rings and his genie, that's
      more,
I would part with them all for to gain you
And live upon Lough Erne Shore.

And when he left the Lough and headed for the heathery moorlands of Mollybreen and Meenatully, the Muses would mingle with the heady wine of the wilderness and inspire such an exquisite song as *Sheila Nee Iyer:*

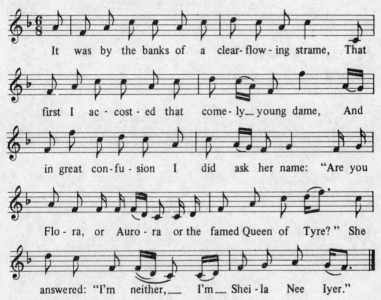

It was by the banks of a clear-flow-ing strame, That
first I ac-cost-ed that come-ly— young dame, And
in great con-fu-sion I did ask her name: "Are you
Flo-ra, or Auro-ra or the famed Queen of Tyre?" She
answered: "I'm neither,— I'm— Shei-la Nee Iyer."

"Go rhyming rogue, let my flocks roam in peace
You won't find amongst them the famed Golden Fleece.
The tresses of Helen, that goddess of Greece,
Have hanked round your heart like a doll of desire
Be off to your spéirbhean," said Sheila Nee Iyer.

"May the sufferings of Sisyphus fall to my share,
And may I the torments of Tantalus bear,
To the dark land of Hades my soul fall an heir
Without linnet in song or a note on the lyre,
If ever I prove false to you, Sheila Nee Iyer.

"O had I the wealth of the Orient store,
All the gems of Peru or the Mexican ore,
Or the hand of a Midas to mould o'er and o'er
Bright bracelets of gold and of flaming saphire,
I would robe you in splendour my Sheila Nee Iyer."

Surely it was a somewhat similar mood that moved the Munster man to pen the delightful *Colleen Rue*.

As— I roved out on a— sum-mer's morn - ing a— spec-u - la - ting most cur-ious-ly, To my sur-prise whom should I spy— but a— rur-al mai - den ap-proaching me I stood a— while in deep med-i - ta - tion, con-tem-pla - ting what I— should do, Till at last re - crui - ting all — my sen-sa - tions I— thus ac - cost - ed the Colleen Rue.

Are you Auroa or the goddess Flora, Artemidora or Venus bright
Or Helen fair beyong compare, whom Paris stole from the Grecian
    sight
O fairest creature you have enslaved me, I'm caplivated in Cupid's
    clew
Your golden sayings are infatuations that have ensnared me, a
    Colleen Rue

Kind sir, be easy and do not tease me; with your false praises most
    jestingly
Your dissimulation and invocation are vaunting praises alluring me
I'm not Aurora or the goddess Flora, but a rural maiden to all men's
    view
Who is here condoling my situation; my appellation — the Colleen
    Rue.

Oh, were I Hector, that noble victor who died a victim to Grecian
    skill
Or were I Paris whose deeds are various an arbitrator on Ida's hill
I'd range through Asia, likewise Arabia, Pennsylvania seeking for you
The burning raygions like sage Orpheus to see your face my sweet
    Colleen Rue.

Perhaps the most charming of all hedge-school-masters'
effusions is that written by one of the bards from the illustrious hedge-school of Tirgarvil in the county of Derry. I got
the song from that fine Ulster traditional singer, Len Graham,
who works a rich vein of song that runs from Magilligan in
Derry through Ballymena and Ballymoney to the Nine Glens
of Antrim.

Des - cend, ye chaste Mu- ses, ye— bards and ye sag - es And
Or - pheus who tamed roar-ing   beasts with his lyre   Ye—
an - cient hist - or - ians that's dead man— y ag - es, I
hope you'll a - wake and my   gen- ius in - spire   Ye
great men of learn-ing lend me ap - pro - ba - tion, Ye
gods and phi - lo - so - phers lend me   your aid   . In—
praise of— a   fair one I— leave in this na - tion, She's the
bright star of Er - in   and the   Flower of— Gor -tade.

O were I as Homer that prince of the writers
Who sang of Athenians and Spartans of old
Could I paint with the skill of a Roman inditer
The fame of this fair one can never be told
Penelope, Venus, Diana and Flora,
Whose beauty and chastity never can fade
Fair Helen, Lucretia and famous Aurora
Even these wouldn't equal the Flower of Gortade.

Unrivalled she stands 'mid the daughters of Erin
For style and for beauty none can her excel
On the fourth of September my bark she is steering
Far far from the spot I did formerly dwell
The consorts of Hector who are mentioned in story
Susanna whose virtue is still undecayed
Queen Dido who dwelt with her soverign in the glory
Even these wouldn't equal the Flower of Gortade

Adieu to old Erin, the land of my childhood
Where luxury, wealth and magnificence rove
No more I'll traverse o'er the plain and the wildwood
Or list to the mavis that sings in the grove
And if to Columbia God send me safe over
I'll write a few lines to my own comrade maid
Who along with her sister and my dear old mother
Await my return once again to Gortade

"Things have changed and not for the better. I mind myself when I was a lump of a cub, and that's not a hundred years ago, we grew our own grain, ground our own meal, killed our own pig and made our own drink. Damn it! wasn't there a still in every other house in this townland and when the men were coping hard lea or banking turf in Derrarona bog, weren't the weemin running a heat of poteen over in the sallys near the seskin.

"And if you wanted a grouse or a woodcock, you ris early and went up the Cordoss Crua or over by the Finn Hills and bagged your brace of birds. There was no one to put to you or from you only Tit McGee, the gamekeeper, and poor Tit soon got tired chasing you over rough ground.

"Do you know what I'm goin' to tell you; every barn had eight or nine two-hundred bags of meal grown at home and ground in the mill, and that didn't count the corn kept for the fowl and the beasts! What oats are in this house now? Kate, could you tell us?"

His sister went over to a cupboard in the corner and brought forth a quarter-stone packet of speedicook oats and held it aloft.

"There you are man! That proves my point. And that's what the sputniks and televisions have brought us to! Then take the spud. Man dear, the spuds we grew then were meat and kitchen for any white man. Not like the watergalls that's agrowin' now, that you can scoot out of their skins.

"We hadn't much money then but we didn't need it, we had our own homespun sport. Your house was a great rambling house. So was this one. Many a good highland fling and four-hand reel was flaked out on that floor. Sure you mind it yourself, Paddy?"

I nodded assent, for Mick Hernon was in full flight back into the past and who was I to ground him.

"We were happy and content then", he mused. "Do you know that tune, Cathal, *Contentment Is Wealth?* There's a lot of truth in the title." My son Cathal signified that he knew the tune and both men struck up and played it together and many other until three o'clock in the morning.

The fiddles were then put away and the chatting began in earnest. I inquired if the wee people were as plentiful as they used to be in our part of the country.

"No, they're not Paddy", he told me firmly, "It's more's the pity! Since the poteen-making quit they have just melted away. They tell me it took the spirits to keep them alive."

If poteen was so potent surely it inspired the poets. Isn't *The Loyal Blackbird* or *The Blackbird of Mullaghmore* one of the many songs in praise of stills and poteen-making?

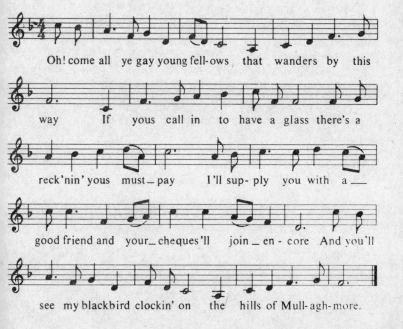

Well it's for your loyal blackbird she's of the best of game
Her offspring are well proven in America, France and Spain
Her cheque has gained her credit on many's the foreign shore
And now she's sitting clocking on the hills of Mullaghmore.

Well it's for your loyal blackbird, they didn't use her well
And the hardships that she underwent there's no mortal tongue can
    tell
When her cage door was opened they rushed them in a score
And they put my bird from clocking on the hills of Mullaghmore.

So our blackbird's going to leave us now which grieves the neighbours
    all
And I hope she'll have good fortune until on her we do call
She's going over yonder mountain for the rest in a fine still
And she'll spend her summer season at the foot of the Sheep Hill.

And our blackbird's coming home again but not to the same place
And I hope your friends and neighbours will not bring her to disgrace
And the lovely lark and linnet and the thrush will join encore
For to welcome home our blackbird to the hills of Mullaghmore.

This song was collected by Seán O Boyle from Owen
McAteer of Hilltown in the county of Down during nineteen
hundred and fifty-two. The singer was reluctant to give Seán
any information as to where he himself had got the song.
When pressed, he at length told the truth: "I was courtin' a
girl", he said, "and I stole it out of her pocket!"

I had heard old Johnnie McGuire of Derrarona mention
the song but he insisted that the proper name was *The Loyal
Blackbird.*

My mother, God rest her, had no time for Bacchus. In fact she was a teetotaler all the days of her life, but there was one fine drinking song she sang occasionally, although with a certain degree of diffidence. It is called:

DRINKING STRONG WHISKEY
One night I being tipsy from drinking strong whiskey
The bumpers were passed right merrily round
The toasts they were listed and no one resisted
And Terry his fiddle did cheerfully sound
I being apprehended by Aristo Reaper
And straight to the raygions of dead men did go
And as sure as you're there I did swear by John Payton
O that I would have the old napper from Joe.

Chorus

Right fol the dee arl, right fol the dee arl,
Right fol the dee arl, right fol the dee ay
Right fol the dee arl, right fol the dee arl
Right fol the dee arl, right fol the dee ay.

I'll have you be civil, or were you the divil
You'll have to come down with me to the road
No wonder you're so weary in a spot that's so dreary
Down by these old walls where he makes his abode
I wonder if souls who go up to heaven
E'er back to the regions of mortals do stray
Or if they were sentenced to Pluto's dark prison
I'm sure old Cerebus wouldn't let them away.

Chorus

"Cullaville for wrestling!" exclaimed the man from South Armagh as he stood on a high spink of the Rocky Mountains and watched the grizzly bear he had just strangled hurtle down the rock face to the ravine below. He had been on his keeping for some time, as the result of his activities with the Whiteboys, and at length had made his way to the land of the free on board a friendly ship.

In those old times it seems, South Armagh was a favourite haunt of secret societies. Whiteboys, Ribbonmen, Defenders and the Knights of Saint Patrick all flourished there, and although they were oath-bound organizations pledged to secrecy, it was customary to muster now and then in the open. There was a two-fold purpose served by such an exercise. The smouldering fires were re-fuelled and fanned in the hearts of the Gael and the daylights were scared out of Clann Wullie.

Of such a nature was the meeting described in the rousing old song from Forkhill called *When Saint Peter's Day was a dawning,* collected by Seán O Boyle from a cobbler by the name of Peter Reilly, who lived in the South Armagh territory, some time during July 1952.

It is a song nearer the Gaelic tradition than any known to me. Indeed Peadar O Duirnín could have written it himself if ever he stooped to composition in the borrowed Béarla.

The melody is most interesting. It is an amalgam of *Cáitlín Triail, Saint Patrick's Day* and that jaunty little jig, *The Bunch Of Green Rushes That Grew On The Brim.* It is one of my favourite songs in English. Listen to it.

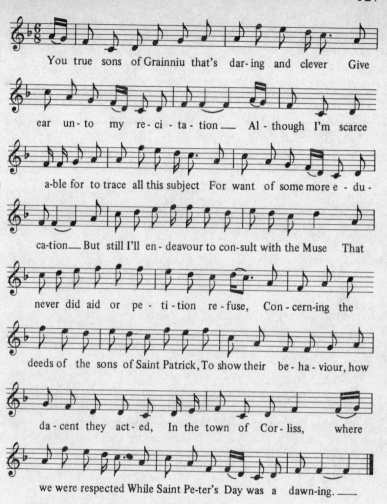

You true sons of Grainniu that's dar-ing and clever Give
ear un-to my re-ci-ta-tion___ Al-though I'm scarce
a-ble for to trace all this subject For want of some more e-du-
ca-tion___ But still I'll en-deavour to con-sult with the Muse That
never did aid or pe-ti-tion re-fuse, Con-cern-ing the
deeds of the sons of Saint Patrick, To show their be-ha-viour, how
da-cent they act-ed, In the town of Cor-liss, where
we were respected While Saint Pe-ter's Day was a dawn-ing.___

The number appeared, in Corliss we hear,
It was ten thousand bodies in station
With their helmets of steel, bright guns and broad shields
For to free and protect all this nation
Each body assembled soon formed in a line
They were dressed in all grandeur for to take the prize
They would fight till they'd die or they'd win satisfaction
For Island Magee, for the Boyne or for Aughrim

For the debts that were due for the blood of the martyrs
While Saint Peter's Day was a dawning
Our drums they did beat and our trumpets did sound
The Harp of old Ireland palyed *Orange Lie Down*
And the Brunswicks awoke in this nation all round
And the Black Hare of Luther no longer was sleeping
For she quickly arose, between mourning and weeping,
And through hedges and holes at us they were peeping
While Saint Peter's Day was a dawning

At Fetherna Bush these parties were dressed
In silk scarves and green sashes tied round them
With their helmets of steel, bright guns and broad shields
Their bugles and trumpets were soundin'
By re-inforcements our lines they did fill
With all the bright heroes around Cullaville
The spectators did gaze and with wonder did fill
For to see us approaching, as we all marched together
With our blooming cockades, our neat plume and feather
We carried the sway, took the pride of all other
While Saint Peter's Day was a dawning

You true sons of Grainniu, Milesians so pure
Who sprang from the Rocks of Gadelus
Who was bit by the snakes and by Moses was cured
And green was the spot he was healed on
Patriarch David was chosen our king
Who Goliath the giant, he slew with a sling
And down from his race our Virgin did spring
Who bore the Messiah and trampled the serpent
That came to the Garden where Adam was tempted
And His blood he did spill for to have sin exempted
While Saint Peter's Day was a dawning.

Well it's now to conclude, my advice to you
Is to tear down all rotten foundations
And banish this crew that our land did pollute
And corrupted our true ordinations
We'll raise up a storm and chase them away
All the informers since King Harry's day
And all other tribes that with them would say
We'll send them asailing, all putrid and carr'on
To some other island that's fruitless and barren
For this one was promised to Moses and Aaron
While Saint Peter's Day was a dawning

There is no other composition in the whole corpus of our traditional song that captures the ferocity and mórtas cine of the Gael as this one does.

Resembling it in metrical construction is a song known once as *Saint Patrick's Day in the Morning,* but alas! there is only one verse extant. It was sung by my songmaster, Michael Gallagher, but what a pity my mother could recall only one verse.

SAINT PATRICK'S DAY IN THE MORNING
When he came to our shore, our land was spread o'er
With witchcraft and dark necromancy
Deludes I may say with such dark, evil ways
As were pleasing to Beelzebub's fancy
This champion of Christ did their magic expel
These imps of perdition he did them repell
Their worship he stopped and their idols they fell
And he showed them the path that would lead to Mount Sion
The right way to live and the true way to die in
And none would be lost who were patronised by him
On Saint Patrick's Day in the morning.

If the Gael could claim kindred with the great King David surely the Freemasons' claim to descent from the master-builders of King Solomon's temple is equally valid. This world-wide secret society claims to meet man on the level and treat him on the square. Laudable sentiments indeed, and it seems our true Freemason practises what he preaches.

Down on his right knee, his left hand on the Book of the Law, two white wands held cross-like over his head, he takes the oath of secrecy and faith: "to hail, conceal and never reveal the hidden mysteries of the fellowship."

And if the Mason's white apron is a symbol as glorious to him as the Ark of The Covenant was to the Isrealites, is it any wonder that the signs and rituals of the Order should inspire a poet to song in spite of all the secrecy?

Thus we have *The Grand Templars' Song.* It is conceded readily enough that the Knights of the Grand Templars were part of the army of noble-minded men that repaired to Palestine during the Great Crusades to protect the Holy places from the infidel hordes. However, the poet leaves no doubt in the minds of his listeners as to the identity of the Grand Templars he salutes. They are members of a Lodge of Royal Arch Masonry be their badge that of the Taw, the Key or the Cross-Keys. Here is *The Grand Templars' Song:*

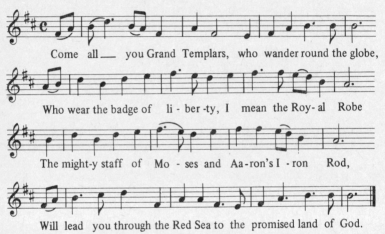

Come all— you Grand Templars, who wander round the globe,

Who wear the badge of li - ber -ty, I mean the Roy- al Robe

The might-y staff of Mo - ses and Aa-ron's I - ron Rod,

Will lead you through the Red Sea to the promised land of God.

> And when I think of Moses, it causes me to blush
> That day upon Mount Horeb where he spied the Burning Bush
> His sandals he cast off his feet, his staff he threw away
> And as a pilgrim he did wander until his dying day
>
> Noah was upright in the sight of the Lord
> He loved the Free Masons and kept the Royal Word
> Twas he built the first ship and planted the first vine
> And his glory in heaven, like an angel's doth shine
>
> Three dazzling lights I saw, that filled me with surpise
> And gazing all around me, I heard a dreadful noise
> The serpent passed me by, I bent unto the ground
> And with joy, peace and gladness, the Secret I found

The Grand Templars' Song I learnt from my mother, who in turn picked it up from the Tullaghasson troubadour, William Monaghan. Neither of them were Freemasons.

Now here is another masonic song I got from my good friend and fine singer, Len Graham. He learnt it from Sandy

Given of Dundooan, in the county of Derry. It is a noble song with a wealth of imagery and a richness of biblical allusion that equals the grandeur of the great hedge-school-master compositions. Hear ye this!

THE KNIGHT TEMPLAR'S DREAM

As Morpheus my senses in slumber did drown
I dreamt I was climbing Horeb's holy mound
Where Moses was chosen Grand Master in love
By the Great architect in Heaven above
With trembling fear and wonder I did gaze
To see a bush aburning all by a mighty blaze
My bones they did shudder and feeble was my frame
When a dreadful fiery serpent right forward to me came

I looked at death approaching with terror, dread and grief
Then called on Goodness to grant me some relief
When to my astonishment a voice unto me said
"Come, take up the serpent and do not be afraid."
I then became a pilgrim to travel night and day
I took the Rod of God to guide me on my way
Over high hill and mountains, bound for the Temple bright
Till I came to Jerusalem, that city of delight

I saw the Knights of Malta in shining armour bright
Surround the Sons of Darkness that cast away the light
I crossed the river Jordan and Jericho likewise
To lovely Mount Sion where sweet odours scent the skies
I enlisted as a soldier to fight for Christian liberty
Against the Turk and Heathen and all idolatory
To all our faithful battles Jehovah lent a hand
To Gideon, Beeve and Joshua who caused the sun to stand

I travelled over Mount Arorrat and fair Armeria's land
From that to Enoch's Temple where I saw two pillars grand
I knocked upon the gasper gates admittance there I sought
Through many coloured arches till I found the sacred font
With torches burning round me in one continuous blaze
Where I saw the mystery and on it in awe did gaze
When to my astonishment two fiery dragons came
And at the height of my surprise I woke out of my drame

Ribbonman and Ribbonism have also got favourable mention in song. Perhaps the most poignant and dramatic of this genre is *The Ribbon Blade,* a song that records the fate of one Mick Sheridan from Killala. The tune is a variant of *The Flower of Sweet Strabane*

> I am a Roman Catholic, Mick Sheridan is my name
> From the chapel in Killala on a Sunday as I came
> Whom should I spy to my surprise, but Yeomen on parade
> Said the one unto the other: "Yonder comes a Ribbon Blade."
>
> They all then gathered round me, and ordered me to stand
> I didn't know the reason why they gave such strict command
> At length bold Colston up he spoke and this to them he said:
> "Mick Sheridan from Killala he commands the Ribbon Blades."
>
> They marched me off to Ballina and laid me in a jail
> Where I lay cold and hungry my sad fate to bewail
> And all that time I only saw but one true Irish maid
> O that goodness may reward her for she loved a Ribbon Blade
>
> They offered me high wages to make discovery
> Or else that they would banish me to my sad destiny
> The answer that I gave to them was this I'm sure I said:
> "I'll be true unto eternity to any Ribbon Blade."
>
> My sisters are at home and they sorrow after me
> My mother she is blind and not one styme can see
> My father cries: "My darling boy do not the name degrade
> For discovery you never make on any Ribbon Blade."
> There's one request I'll ask of you going up yon gallows high
> I hope my loyal comrades will have revenge for me
> That they will have revenge for me in felon clay I'm laid
> And we'll let them know before we go we are ture Ribbon Blades

With that note of defiance Mick Sheridan departed this mortal life to enter the immortal memory of his people.

> The dead who died for Ireland,
> let not their memory die
> But solemn and bright like the stars of night
> may they be enthroned on high.

Nor is the Orange Order without it's corpus of traditional song. We are all familiar with *The Green Grassy Slopes of The Boyne, The Aghalee Heroes* and it's mock heroics and the

jauntiness of that lovely little song, *The Orange Lily O!* However, songs alluding to the ritual and secrets of the Order are
few and far between. Indeed, until 1952 when one William
Coulter sang *The Purple Boy* for Seán O Boyle, it was not
sung outside the Lodge.

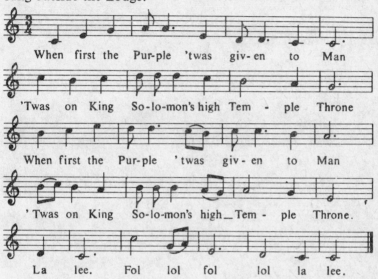

When first the Pur-ple 'twas giv-en to Man
'Twas on King So-lo-mon's high Tem - ple Throne
When first the Pur-ple 'twas giv-en to Man
'Twas on King So-lo-mon's high Tem - ple Throne.
La lee. Fol lol fol lol la lee.

"Now come tell me darling,
  come tell me joy,
Come tell to me, my true
  Purple Boy,
What are those secrets you love
  so sweet?"
"I'm afraid those secrets, them I
  must keep."

Some love the mark, some love
  the blue
But I would die for the scarlet
  too
Those Ribbon rascals I would
  defy
And I'd wear the colours till the
  day I die,

Now I wish, I wish I were a man
That I could join in your Orange
  band
Then all my sorrows would turn
  to joy
'Twould be rolling in the arms of
  my Purple Boy

Now come all young girls that
  choose a man
Choose that Purple boy, if you
  can,
For they're the ones that will
  love you best
For they wear the mark on their
  left breast

Finally here is a song collected by my Uncle Mick in 1953 from Mary Anne McGuire of Kimmet, Pettigo, County Donegal, that, in it's own way, helped to keep the old faith alive during the dark days of persecution. It portrays the plight of a Defender and member of the Church of Rome.

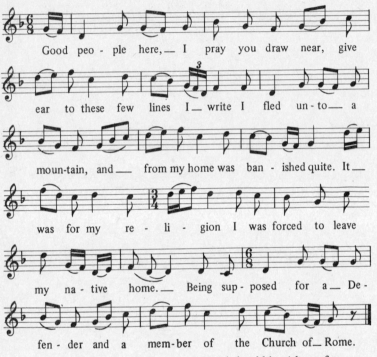

Good peo - ple here, — I pray you draw near, give ear to these few lines I — write I fled un - to — a moun-tain, and — from my home was ban - ished quite. It — was for my re - li - gion I was forced to leave my na - tive home. — Being sup - posed for a — De - fen - der and a mem-ber of the Church of — Rome.

These Luthers black and Calvin crew said they'd banish me from my
    native soil
And leave me here to languish, to languish lonely in exile
Such persecutions we must bear, Our Saviour suffered ten time more
When he died on Calvary, that we might reach that heavenly shore

He cured the lame and raised the dead, and with five loaves and
    fishes two
He fed five thousand faithful, who flocked to hear his gospel true
He gave himself as heavenly food and pledge of great and lasting love
To strengthen and to guide us, triumphant to the joys above

Our holy Church is pure and fair, and she is founded on a Rock
Saint Peter got the keys from Christ to nourish and to feed his flock
Who said he will be with us until that great tremendous day
The Holy Ghost to guide us, how can we ever go astray!

Behold that race of Calvin seed, that wander here and wander there
Still looking for a harbour, no wonder they're in deep despair
Their compass needle it is broke, their topmasts, sails and riggings
    tore
Contrary winds are blowing, they'll never reach that heavenly shore

It was in 1952 that the Hidden Ireland burst forth from the confines of the hearth and let it's light shine before men. Byran McMahon, that master of many arts, began it all a few years before with his *Ballad-Makers' Saturday Night.* Benedict Kiely followed suit with his *Nine Counties Of Ulster,* a series of radio programmes wrought from the rich vein of the Ulster idiom. Comhaltas Ceoltoirí Éireann held it's great Fleadh in Monaghan town.

Seán MacRéamoinn came north with a mobile recording unit to gather material for the Nine Counties series and other traditional radio programmes of his own. Séamus Ennis, another legend in his lifetime, was toiling away in the Gaelic West, in Cork, Kerry, Connemara and that great principality of the O'Donnell known as Tír Chonaill. "Nuair a bhíos i gConamara tráth," was a phrase frequently repeated on Radio Éireann round that ime.

Even the BBC Northern Ireland bestirred itself and sent talent scouts riding east and west and south and north like Lares Proseno long ago, to summon an array of traditional singers, musicians and story-tellers to the microphone.

The auditions were very enjoyable and as a result of my attendance at one of them in Enniskillen I was subsequently offered a contract and, in the fullness of time, gave my first live broadcast. Previously some of my songs had been used in Radio Éireann programmes but they had been recorded in advance.

I sang *Róisín Dubh, The Mountain Streams where the Moorcocks Crow, Lough Erne Shore* and *Wee Paddy Molloy* in that order. At least one Ulsterman took the pains to listen to the short programme and, in the course of a couple of days, he wrote me a letter of congratulations, and mentioned that himself and a Londoner would be collecting songs and

music during July and August and he requested permission
to call on me. Permission was readily granted and so I met
Seán O Boyle, scholar and leading authority on Irish traditional song both in Irish and in English. His programmes
entitled *Music On The Hearth* and his co-operation with Peter
Kennedy, Spike Hughes and Séamus Ennis in the long-running
BBC Light Programme series, *As I Roved Out,* coupled with
his publications, notably *The Irish Song Tradition,* has made
his name a household word throughout the Gaelic and English-
speaking worlds.

Thus began a friendship that grew firmer with the passage
of the years. I can well recall a bardic night spent with Seán,
his father Charles, Liam Andrews and Peter Kennedy, in
Belfast that year. We sang and swapped versions of songs all
night until the grey daylight was peeping in. Charles was a
great admirer of my mother's style of singing and I can see
him still, listening intently to her recordings of *The Forsaken
Bride* and *The Lowlands of Holland* that Seán and Peter had
made a few days before.

It was during that night Charles sang *The Greenwood
Laddie,* in that quiet, dignified and utterly inimitable style
of his.

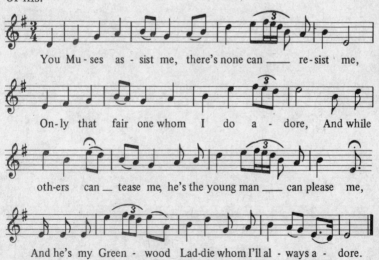

You Mu-ses as-sist me, there's none can ___ re-sist me,

On-ly that fair one whom I do a-dore, And while

oth-ers can ___ tease me, he's the young man ___ can please me,

And he's my Green-wood Lad-die whom I'll al-ways a-dore.

If you had seen my dearest, with eyes of the clearest
His cheeks like the red blood that's new-dropped in snow
He is neat, tall and slender and his hands soft and tender
He is my Greenwood Laddie wherever he go

My parents, my darling, they slight you with scorn
Because you've no riches all wrapped up in store
But the more that they slight you, the more I'll invite you
To be my Greenwood Laddie till time is no more.

For if I had the wealth of the East and West Indies
Or if I had the gold of the African Shore
Or if I could gain thousands, I'd lie on your bosom
You'll be my Greenwood Laddie I'll always adore

It's down in yon bower, we spent many's the long hour
A-plucking the flowers in his company
It was his stolen kisses gave me my heart's wishes
He'll be my Greenwood Laddie wherever he be.

Charles also sang versions of *The Verdant Braes of Screen*
and *The Flower of Magherally O,* and indeed many other fine
Ulster songs.

Liam Andrews gave us *Lovely Willie,* a song I fell in love
with at first sound. Here it is:

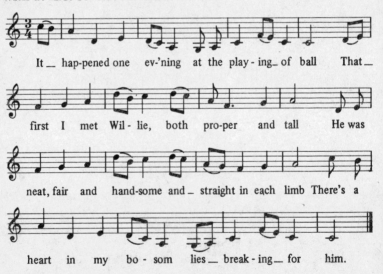

It — hap-pened one ev-'ning at the play-ing— of ball That —
first I met Wil-lie, both pro-per and tall He was
neat, fair and hand-some and— straight in each limb There's a
heart in my bo-som lies— break-ing— for him.

"Oh, won't you come with me a small piece of the road
To see my father's dwelling and place of abode?"
He knew by her looks and her languishing eye
That he was the young man she had cherished most high

"There's a spot in my father's garden, lovely Willie", said she,
"Where lords, dukes and earls they wait upon me
But when they are sleeping in their long, silen rest
I'll go with you, Lovely Willie, you're the boy I love best."

Her father being listening, in ambush he lay
To hear the fond words that these lovers did say
And with a sharp rapier he pierced her love through
And the innocent blood of her darling he drew

The grave was got ready, lovely Willie laid in
The Mass it was chanted to clear his soul of sin
"And it's oh, honoured father, you may say as you will
But the innocent blood of my love you did spill"

"And I will go off to some far country
Where I will know no one and no one knows me
And it's there I will wander till I close my eyes in death
For you, lovely Willie, you're the boy I love best"

Exactly one year later Seán O Boyle, Peter Kennedy and myself again met together and set out in quest of John Simie (Simon) Doherty, the unique travelling fiddler and living legend of the Donegal highlands.

It was a fine day in summer. Larks were singing and new-mown meadows burned incense in the sun. At a bend in the road Peter Kennedy stopped and consulted a map.

"Cloghan?", he put the question.

"Over the mountain", I told him, "but we can't take the high road."

"Why?" asked the Londoner.

"It's the way the crow flies!" I gave him back.

So we took the low road through Barnesmore Gap and the Twin-Towns and then followed the River Finn back by shady trout-pool and salmon-leap till we reached the airy little village of Cloghan, tucked away under the oxter of the hills.

"Ye're a wee thing early", Master Campbell remarked as he joined us in the recording car. "John was here last night but sure you weren't due for another couple of days."

"If we're early itself you can put the blame on me", I told him. "I got a hunch yesterday that he might bolt in the latter end and go into hiding in the mountains."

"You could be right", the Master observed, obviously unimpressed.

"We headed back the Glenties road through Fintown but failed to pick up any trace. A Garda Sergeant wheelbarrowing turf to the road informed us that he had taken a branch road towards the Gweebara River around dinner-time of day. We followed his directions.

Slowly we crawled deeper into the Donegal highlands where sheep clung like maggots in the heathery hide of the foothills. We inquired from other turfmen toiling away with asses and creels as we went. Then, as if by magic, a red-haired boy helter-skeltered up on a piebald pony, and blurted out that Uncle John had passed him two hours before.

We had got a strong scent and tracked on enthusiastically. The by-road narrowed to a sheep-track and then we were suddenly brought to an abrupt halt by a huge trunk of bog-oak laid across a gap. Seán O Boyle and myself alighted but strain as we might, the barrier would not budge.

"Wait a minute." The burly figure of the Master was by my side. He advanced and with consummate ease, raised one end of the trunk and let the recording car pass. Recalling Oisín and the raising of the stone, the breaking of the saddle girth and his fall to the ground where he was immediately stricken with extreme old age, I considered it my duty to warn the Master.

"It's alright", he assured me, "like *The Man from God Knows Where* myself and Oisín ride different ways. Sure a fall from Shank's Mare never did any man a deal of harm!"

A mile further on we came to a house. Peter Kennedy noted that the doors of the kitchen and barn had been newly painted. According to him this was a sign that a celebrity was expected. Sure enough a woman emerged from the barn with paint brush and can. "Did you see John Simie pass this way?" Peter Kennedy asked for the umpteenth time that day.

"Troth an' I did", came the reply, "wasn't he in on me before I got the painting finished. He took tay here half-an-hour ago!" Peter hugged the woman tightly, paint-can, paint-brush and all.

We hastened on. Round the next loop we sighted our quarry. There before us was the fiddling prince of the Donegal highlands, striding along freely with his pedlar's pack.

"An Mangaire Súgach", exclaimed Seán O Boyle, visibly moved, and I thought of Cathal Buí Mac Giolla Gunna roaming the roads of Ulster with a thirst for the drink and a grá for the women, and Blind Raftery in the boreens of Connacht scraping away on a bad fiddle, his heart burned to a cinder with the memory of the beauty of Mary Hynes. We had found the last living link with the great wandering minstrels and harpers of the eighteenth century, to whom Rory Dáil Ó Catháin and Denis O Hempsie had passed on the torch through the fiddling of Denis McCabe of Castlecaldwell and, at a later date, the piping of John's own kinsman, An Píobaire Mór, Turlough MacSuibhne of Gweedore.

Below us the broad bosom of the Gweebara billowed away to the sea. "Had he reached the bruagh of the river, and got ferried across Lettermacaward, hilt or hair of him we'd have never seen," declared the Master.

Back in Master Campbell's spacious drawing-room John Doherty was in his element. He tuned Peter Kennedy's fiddle and talked of fiddlers to Seán O Boyle. Glancing down at the four fox-skins on the floor, he announced that he'd play *Seilg A' Mhadaidh Ruaidh,* or *The Fox-chase.* We listened enthralled to the baying of hounds, the echo of hunting horn and the anguished cry of the dying fox in that memorable piece of traditional playing.

He followed on with other famed slow airs. These included *The Harvest Morning* or, in the Gaelic, *Maidin Fhómhair, Easter Snow* and a hauntingly beautiful version of *The Lord Of Mayo.* His own setting of the renowned Jacobite air, *The Blackbird,* followed, both in slow and quick tempo, and to put the crathán on a veritable stack of tunes he gaves us *The Wounded Huzzar,* an English lament once played by Thomas Hardy's father in far-off Dorset. John Doherty's playing of slow airs is mostly in the Gaelic classical tradition.

Today, however, a traditional fiddler's merit is measured more by the manner of his reel playing and so we waited and wondered. We might have spared ourselves the worry.

When he launched out in *The Yellow Heifer, The Glen Road to Carrick, The Ivy Leaf* and *The Nine Points of Knavery,* he put the ancient mariner on us all.

It was only then we realised how inextricably interwoven is the fiddle music of Scotland and the Orkneys and Shetlands with the famed Donegal style. This fact was later confirmed when John went on to play a highland Scottishe and declared his great admiration for James Scot Skinner, the well-known Scottish fiddler.

John talked of his father, who was reputed to be "the king fiddler of them all", to put it in John's own words. "When my father was playing a reel in the right spirit you could hear the top of the bow whistling!" he declared. Try that feat, ye fiddlers of Clare and Kerry.

John Doherty is also a fine singer. At Carrick, where we went to meet his old fiddling friend, Frank Cassidy, we made this discovery. Frank told us an amazing story of the All-Souls Night fiddlers. He himself and his two brothers never played on All-Souls Night in deference to their dear departed ones, but when they had finished making visits in the chapel they made their céili in a neighbouring house.

This All-Souls Night they had céilied to a late bedtime, for it had been a mighty night's story-telling, and as they came up the road from the Teelin side they were stopped dead in their tracks with the most wonderful reel-playing ever heard by mortal ear. "The wee folk", one of them whispered as they tiptoed up the road towards their own home. Then to their utter astonishment, they discovered that the music was coming from their own house. In those days there was no need to lock up when you went out and so the door was on the latch.

Cautiously they crept up to the door and as one lifted the latch noiselessly another grabbed the candle off the table, lit it and held it aloft. The music stopped abruptly but, as the candle-light chased away the shadows, they beheld their three fiddles and bows suspended in mid air near the hearth. As they gazed in wonder, the fiddles and bows once more obeyed the law of gravity, and sank slowly to the floor, landing noiselessly on the flagstones. "Not a fiddle was out of tune!" Frank declared.

"Lord have mercy on the fiddlers in Purgatory", prayed John Doherty, "sure you wouldn't begrudge them their wee session on All-Souls Night!"

It was then he struck up the song *The Old Man Rocking the Cradle* or *Hushaba Cliabhán* to escape from the world of spirits for he doesn't like tales of the supernatural or talk of ghosts.

It — was the other night that I chanced to go rov-ing, Down
by the wee riv-er I jogged a - long I —
heard an old man mak-ing sad la - men - ta - tion A-bout
rock-ing the crad-le, and the child not his own. Hi -
ho hi - ho hi ba - by lie eas - y; Per -
haps your own dad-dy will nev-er be known I'm —
sigh - ing and sob-bing and rock-ing the cradle And
nurs - ing a ba - by that's none of my own.

She goes out every night to a ball or a party
And leaves me here rocking the cradle alone
And it's by the Lord Harry, if ever you marry
You're sure to be rocking the cradle alone *Chorus*
So come all you young men that's inclined to get married
Take my advice, leave the women alone
For it's by the Lord Harry if ever you marry
You're sure to be rocking the cradle alone *Chorus*

This song is reminiscent of the kind composed and sung by Owen Rua O'Sullivan, but how did Owen of the Sweet Mouth get so far north? John sang us a version of *Moorlough Mary* and another most interesting song:

THE THREE O'DONNELLS

As I roved out one morning,
In the merry month of June
As the sun arose on Lough
 Swilly's shores
And everything in bloom
On a primrose bank as I sat
 down
All by a crystal stream
So deep, so deep I fell asleep
And I began to dream.

So it's when we heard of liberty
We let ourselves be known
And were you at that meeting
 boys
That was held in Innishowen
For it's long and long since we
 were bound
But now, thank God, we're free
And if ever we be bound again
We'll fight for liberty

I dreamt I saw a loaded barge
Going floating down the main
With four and twenty Irish boys
To guide her on the stream
It being on her bows stood one
 young man
Who soon alarmed me
Rise up! Rise up! you troubled
 mind
For Gáinne's sons are free.

Here's a health to the three
 O'Donnells
They're a credit to the name
They're a credit to their country
 boys
Both honour, birth and fame
There were two of them made
 clergymen
All in the Church of Rome
Till God himself called one of them
Unto his heavenly home.

Here's a health to Father William boys
Who fought at Waterloo
He fought the French and Spaniards
'Till he made them to subdue
He fought them with his army
'Till he could no longer stand
He was once a bold lieutenant
But he's now our clergyman.

This is a remarkable song having something of the vision poetry of the eighteenth century Gaelic school about it. In actual fact it is an anti-tithe song from Innishowen. The hero whose praises it sings was none other than Father William O'Donnell, the Waterloo Priest, as he is still affectionately referred to in his native Innishowen.

William O'Donnell was born in Cockhill outside Buncrana in 1779. Soon after his birth his father moved to Rushville from which one of his ancestors had been evicted by Colonel Vaughan under the penal code that precluded a Catholic from ownership of a horse above the value of five pounds, if any of his Protestant neighbours took a fancy to the animal.

Young O'Donnell got his primary education from the eminent classical scholar, Tom McColgan, and in 1802 he entered Maynooth College where he completed his philosophical and theological studies.

His health was impaired by college life and, because of this, he was at first unwilling to take orders in the Church. Law and medicine were suggested as alternatives but he declined both professions for conscientious reasons, being an exceedingly honest man.

At the time General Hart had a number of commissions to dispose of among Irish families and he offered an ensigncy to young O'Donnell. It was accepted and he was gazetted to that post in the Twentieth Foot, on 28 March 1811.

He served with the army throughout the Peninsular War with distinction. The following extract from the *Belfast Vindicator* of 31 March 1849, describing a war medal presentation to him, gives a short account of his career during that period. It reads:

This medal records the battles of Vittoria and the Pyrennees. The former was a brillian display of consummate generalship and military prowess which has been crowned with the most complete success over the most scientific and enterprising generals of the age, commanding the most daring intrepid veteran troops. The fruits of which victory were upwards of 150 pieces of cannon and more than 400 waggons of ammunition, with the military chest and all their baggage and provision stores, with many prisoners.

And how fared our hero when he left the King's Armie? In 1818 he was ordained priest and succeeded his priest brother as administrator of Upper and Lower Fahan and Desertegney, where he remained until 1829. During that time he was again called on to join the army, which he agreed to do only in the capacity of chaplain to the forces. When the authorities refused to grant him these terms, he sold his commission and severed his connection with military life. In 1829 he was appointed Parish Priest of Clonmany.

Now, how else did all the King's horses and all the King's men reward Father William for his heroism and feats of valour on the Plains of Waterloo?

In 1839 they arrested him for arrears of tithe that had accumulated on his property and lodged him in Lifford jail, although he had been legally advised to resist payment of this outrageous impost! Some good friends paid the iniquitous dues, so that his sojourn in prison was not inordinately long. His home-coming was made the occasion of a triumphal march by the people of Strabane, Derry and Innishowen, with bands, banners and torchlight procession.

As parish priest he enlarged the old chapel, built a tower and installed a bell. An advocate of temperance and a promoter of popular education, he erected and furnished five schools in different parts of the parish. He died in Clonmany at the age of 77 years and is buried in the family burying ground at Cockhill.

Clonmany parish would seem to have had it's fair share of clergymen brothers. During the first half of the seventeenth century, in the townland of Claar, between Moville and Redcastle, there lived a man named McLaughlin, of the royal line of the Kings of Ireland.

He had two sons, Domhnall and Peter. These were destined for the Catholic priesthood. Tradition tells us their vessel was shipwrecked on the voyage to the continent and that they were driven in on the English coast.

An English noble befriended them and offered to have them educated in one of the English universities if they would conform to the established Church. Domhnall, in a moment of weakness, yielded to the tempter, and accepted the offer. Peter, being a true McLaughlin, sternly refused. He continued his journey to the continent, entered a Catholic seminary and became a priest. Domhnall, on the other hand, became a minister of King Harry's establishment.

Time passed and by a singular coincidence, one became parish priest and the other became vicar of the parish of Clonmany. Their circumstances were poles apart. Domhnall had a large, well-built church but a congregation of only three members. Peter had a congregation of thousands of souls but their only places of worship were the Mass Rock altars by the seashore or a flag at the mountain top. Domhnall was nicknamed Domhnall Gorm.

The brothers held but little communication with each other and both lived to a ripe old age. Domhnall died first in 1711. Peter wept unceasingly for his black-sheep brother and soon followed him to the grave. Both men were poets and wits. Many of their sallies and repartees are still cherished in the folk-memory of the people.

On one occasion Domhnall was going down to his church and Peter, returning from the celebration of Sunday Mass, met him on the way. "That's it", commented Domhnall, "one going over the other coming back."

"Not so", Peter corrected him, "one going up the other going down."

Their mother lived for many years after Domhnall's appointment to the rectory and not infrequently gave vent to her grief at his fall from the Old Faith in the eloquence of the poetry of her native tongue. Here is an English translation of a fragment of a caoineadh she composed that conveys to some degree, the heart-ache and agony she endured:

Can it e'er be spoken how my heart is broken
By thy fall Ó Domhnaill from the Ancient Faith
With less of sorrow could I view tomorrow
My lost one herding on the mountain brown
Than strange doctrines teaching
and new tenets preaching
At yon lordly window
in his silken gown

So you see John Doherty is not only a musical link with

the great harpers of Ulster, but also one who can evoke memories of the poets, priests and warriors of the past.

But all good things must come to an end and so the evening of the third day found us on the road that borders Lough Finn, dancing to that rollicking old reel, *The Heathery Breezes* played by John Doherty. Peter Kennedy inquired if he would change his way of life and come over to reside with him in London.

"No", John told him firmly, "here I have the mountains" and his gaze swept away to the towering peaks. "Besides there's a fiddle in every other house."

We parted. He strode across the valley, the purple dusk wrapping itself around him like a royal robe.

On that tour we also met Simie and Mickie Doherty, two brothers of John. Both played the fiddle. Simie lost his life in a fire at his little level-crossing house in Ballinamore near Fintown. I never saw so many fiddles hung in any kitchen as adorned the walls of Simie's abode. The evening we called he was shearing a patch of oats and had cut his finger with the sickle. As he started to play the fiddle the bandage became undone and, with the pressure on the strings, bleeding began again. "Bandages are no use", he declared and reaching up to the rafters, he drew down a cobweb and staunched the blood.

I recall he played a number of old reels in different setting to those of John. Then to finish he played the *High Level* "in reverse" as he termed it.

Subsequently we met Mickie in an old house he occupied with his wife at Meetinghouse Street, Stranorlar. Some years later, he moved to a new house in a scheme provided by Donegal County Council for old age pensioners across the way. He has since died.

Mickie was a beautiful storyteller and was adept at creating the proper atmosphere for a tale. He played some reels in perfect time and then switched to slow airs.

"Did you ever hear that air, *The Twisting of the Rope* or *Casadh an tSúgáin?*" he inquired. Seán O Boyle said that he had heard it right enough but asked Mickie to play his version

of the tune. "Now before I play it", Mickie told us, "you'll
have to hear the story."

"O aye, it's a strange story but it's a true one", he began,
"the woman who gets the better of a fiddler needs to be up
early in the morning.

"There was this fiddler and he was after coming from a
dance and he had a long way to go. It came on a very stormy
night and there was only one house on the lonesome road he
had to travel and no one living in it only two women by themselves. It's likes the man of the house had passed away some
time before. So in he went and sat down. After a while he
axed them if he could stay till morning, that he was cold and
tired and had long way to go. He would like to have daylight
with him to travel through the storm and big wind, the way
that he'd have better courage.

"'Well no", says the girl, 'you can't stop here, for there's
no man about the house. There's only me and my mother
and so you can't stop. If there was a man about the house it
would make no difference; but it wouldn't look nice for us
to keep a strange man here. What would the neighbours say
tomorrow morning?'

"'Och! well', says he, 'I'll do you no harm till morning.' So
they seen they couldn't get him out, you know, so they both
studied and hit on a plan. The old lassie went out and she
fetched in an arm of hay. She says to the fiddler 'Are you
any good at twisting them grass ropes, or', says she, 'did you
ever twist a rope in your life?'

"'Indeed an' indeed an' I could twist, twist, twist a rope
from here to Malin!' he stuttered, in a great rage, for his pride
had been stung.

"'Well, do you know', says she, 'we've a lock of ropes to
twist. There's a fine sheeg of hay out there in the haggard
and I'm afraid the big wind might toss it. I'd like to get a
lock of ropes made and tied on it while you're here. I'll let
them out and you can twist', and she reached him the trawhook from aback of a rib in the roof. He had the fiddle hung
on an inside button of his big coat and he left it there.

"He catched the trawhook and joined to twist. 'Twist on,

twist on", she encouraged him, 'ye boyo, out the door you go and away on down the street. I would like to make a good long rope.' So he twisted away and twisted away and twisted away and went backways out the open door and away down the street. When the daughter got him well away from the door she banged it shut and barred and bolted it.

"'Myeo!' says the fiddler, throwing the trawhook and rope from him. He catched the fiddle and hunkering down in the shelter of the old seal-foscaidh that was rickled up outside the door, he composed and played the tune now known as *The Twisting of the Rope.*"

Here is my own translation of the original, Casadh an tSúgáin:

THE TWISTING OF THE ROPE
What sea cat curse, or worse, did drive me to this place
And the girls I left behind refined and full of grace
I went inside, with pride, all full of love and hope
But the hag she forced me out with the twisting of the rope.

Chorus

If you are mine, be mine oh! bright love of my heart!
If you are mine be mine 'till stars from heaven start
If you are mine entwine your life as wife with me
Your love with mine enshrine for all enternity

I am drunk, and more's the shame and blame that's blighting me
My friends would have my life or wife a witch on me
Her crubach cows that browse, arouse in me no hope
They are bacán-bound, and wound around with booragh rope

If the cat had dower, each hour a king would kiss it's mouth
But the other cat has foes and Arctic snows for scouth
That shakings of the bag of hag last night was wed
And how many fine girls waste for taste of man in bed

I can plough and hoe and mow and sow seeds in the ground
I can drive the cows where clover and green grass may be found
I can shoe the noblest steed, fit mount for prince or Pope
But the hag she drove me out with the twisting of the rope

Joseph Campbell, Herbert Hughes and Padraic Colum were members of a literary circle that frequented the Kilmacrennan district during the early years of Irish literary revival in the borrowed tongue. Near Doon Rock, the spot where An Dálach, The O'Donnell, was crowned clan chief in the days before any Saxon bodach attempted to rule in Royal Donegal, tradition says these earnest young men held their courts of poetry.

It was there Hughes collected that beautiful air, *The Belfast Maid,* where it had survived in wordless isolation for the Lord knows how long. Collaborating with him, Campbell wrote the words of *My Lagan Love* and together they gave us an art song that is so akin to the idiom of the people that it is frequently mistaken for a traditional song. No greater tribute could be paid to the Kilmacrennan collaborators.

It matters not an iota that down in Ballinasloe in county Galway they sing a particularly grizzly murder ballad to the same air or, shall we say, a setting of it. Hughes and Campbell were first in the field with the tune and, indeed, the song, so to them the credits must go.

On one occasion, when Colum had returned from a sitting of the court near the Rock of Doon, he sat down and wrote the world-famous song, *She Moved through the Fair.* It too, has passed into the mainstream of traditional song.

It is arguable if Colum's delightful poem-song is in fact an improvement on the original traditional song that I had the good fortune to collect in Clonkillymore, Kilmacrennan, beside the Rock of Doon in 1960, together with my good friend, Hugh McGovern.

It was sung by Barney McGarvey who was then eighty-six years old and has since gone to God. Although the voice was but an echo of what it must have been when he was in his prime, his very distinctive singing style put the come hither on all of us that memorable night.

We were in the home of Mrs. Brigid McGinty and Barney was in good spirits. Barney called his song, *I Once Had a True-Love.*

I once had a sweet-heart, I loved her so well
I loved her far better than my tongue could tell
Her parents they slight me for my want of gear
So adieu to you Molly, since you are not here
I dreaméd last night that my true-love came in
So softly she came that her feet made no din
She steppéd up to me and this she did say
It will not be long love, till our wedding day

Or if I was a fisher down by the sea-side
And my love was a salmon coming in with the tide
I would stretch my net wide and my love I'd ensnare
I own that I love you, I vow and declare
Or if I was a blackbird and had wings to fly
It's on my love's bosom this night I would lie
In a grove of green laurels I'd lay my love down
And with my strong wings I would her surround

O if I was in yonder valley where the small birds do sing
And no one to be near me there I'd cry my fill
Since the notion has took me to make my own will
Sure my own rod beats sorest and does hurt me still
So adieu to you Molly, adieu to you dear
And fare you well darling since you are not here
In a grove of green bushes I will make my moan
And I'll think of you Molly when I am alone

Now there is another song which was a great favourite with my mother that, to some degree, resembles Colum's *She Moved through the Fair.* In fact the first verse is identical. One is tempted to ask who was plundering? Not the folk-poets surely! A version of this song appeared in the Sam Henry collection but my mother's tune and indeed some of the words are quite different. Here it is:

My— young love said— to— me: "My— moth-er won't mind
And my fa - ther won't slight you for— your lack of kind."
And she went a - way from me, and this she did say:
"Oh— it will not— be— long love till— our wed-ding day."

She went away from me and moved through the fair
Where hand-slapping dealers' loud shouts rent the air
The sunlight around her did sparkle and play
Saying "It will not be long love till our wedding day"

When dew falls on meadow and moths fill the night
When glow of the greesagh on hearth throws half-light
I'll slip from the casement and we'll run away
And it will not be long love till our wedding day

According to promise at midnight he rose
But all that he found was the downfolded clothes
The sheets they lay empty 'twas plain for to see
And out of the window with another went she

Yes, love is a killing thing, without any doubt. This fact is brought home to us forcibly by a charming song my mother used to sing many years ago. It goes by the name of *Bonnie Tavern Green*

The first time that I met my love it __ was in __ Ta - vern __
Green   And __ I would wish with   all __ my __ heart her
face I'd never __ seen.   It   was her smil-ing glanc-es   that __
wound - ed   my __ heart   sore   For   I   being sick __ and
bad __ with love   till   I   could love ___ no   more.

O love it is a killing thing I hear the people say
And for to love and not be loved it would drive one astray
For to be sick and bad in love, and not to mend again
False heart, false heart must I die of love, and naught to end my pain

I wish my love was a nightingale, sitting on yon garden wall
And I to be a drop of dew, down on her breast I'd fall
Then into my love's arms, all with great sport and play
And we'd rowl about a whole winter's night, and never think long
      for day

If I was queen of England as Queen Anne was long ago
Many and precious jewels to my love Iwould send o'er
She never would want money while I would reign as queen
For many a pleasant day I spent all round sweet Tavern Green

In 1953 traditional singers all over Ulster began rummaging in the folk memory of the people to recall and resurrect songs that had been interred in the tomb of time for many years. This was due mainly to the energy of Seán O Boyle whose enthusiasm rubbed off on all of us.

My mother was able to remember two verses and a fragment of the *Green Fields of Canada,* but I had to wait patiently for a further ten years before I could extract the full five verses and chorus from her failing memory. Here it is given for the first time in it's entirety:

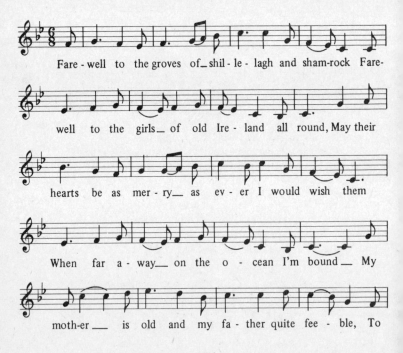

Fare - well to the groves of shil - le - lagh and sham-rock Farewell to the girls of old Ire - land all round, May their
hearts be as mer - ry as ev - er I would wish them
When far a - way on the o - cean I'm bound My
moth-er is old and my fa - ther quite fee - ble, To

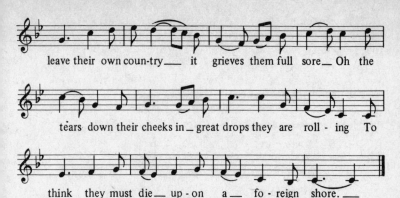

leave their own coun-try__ it grieves them full sore__ Oh the

tears down their cheeks in __ great drops they are roll - ing To

think they must die__ up - on a __ fo - reign shore. __

But what matter to me where my bones may be buried
If in peace and contentment I can spend my life
O the green fields of Canada they daily are blooming
There I'll find an end to my misery and strife *Chorus*

So it's pack up your sea stores, consider no longer
Twelve dollars a week isn't very bad pay
With no taxes or tithes to devour up your wages
When you're on the green fields of Americay

The lint dams are dry and the looms all lie broken
The coopers are gone and the winders of creels
Away o'er the ocean go journeymen tailors
And fiddlers who flaked out the old mountain reels
But I mind the time when old Ireland was flourishing
When lots of her tradesmen did work for good pay
But since our manufactures have crossed the Atlantic
Sure now we must follow to Americay. *Chorus*

Farewell to the dances in homes now deserted
When tips struck the lightening in splanks from the floor
The paving and crigging of hobnails on flagstones
The tears of the old folk and shouts of encore
For the landlords and bailiffs in vile combination
Have forced us from hearthstone and homestead away
May the crowbar brigade all be doomed to damnation
When we're on the green fields of Americay. *Chorus*

The timber grows thick on the slopes of Columbia
With Douglas in grandeur two hundred feet tall
The salmon and sturgeon dam streamlet and river
And the high Rocky Mountains look down over all
On the prairie and plain sure the wheat waves all golden
The maple gives sugar to sweeten your tay
You won't want for corn cob way out in Saskatchwan
When you're on the green fields of Americay. *Chorus*

And if you grow weary of pleasure and plenty
Of fruit in the orchard and fish from the foam
There's health and good hunting 'way back in the forests
Where herds of great moose and wild buffalo roam
And it's now to conclude and to finish my ditty
If ever friendless Irishman chances my way
With the best in the house I will greet him in welcome
At home on the green fields of Americay. *Chorus*

Of all the songs recollected in the tranquility of that year
perhaps the most interesting was *The White Steed*. Now it is
not clear whether this noble beast was the one ridden by
Niamh An Chinn Óir that whisked Oisín away to Tír na nÓg
and the one from which he fell at a later date with such tragic
consequences.

I give it here and I trust it will give the scholars material to
sharpen their tusks on for many a long day. The tune is
Bean an Fhir Rua.

THE WHITE STEED
My horse he was white although at first he was grey
He took great delight in travelling by night and by day
His travels were great if I could but the half of them tell
He was rode in the Garden by Adam the day that he fell

When banished from Eden he strayed and has since lost his way
With all his fatigues it's no wonder my horse he is grey
At the time of the Flood he was rode on by many a spark
And his courage was great when Noah took him into the ark

At the Babylon Plains he conquered that part of the globe
And all his fatigue it would weary the patience of Job
At the battle of Issus my horse he was first in the fray
And with bold Alexander commander he carried the day

My horse got no ease from fatigue when his rider did fall
He was mounted again by brave Scipio who did him extoll
On that great day at Zama fierce Hannibal fled in dismay
And the Captains of Carthage my horse threw them into the say.

That year too was the first time I went dapping. My teachers
were my good friends the McGarans and it was from one of
these encounters with the big trout of Lower Lough Erne
came the urge to write the dapping poem. Here it is:

THE FLY IS UP!
A ploughman pauses in the loam
His team of horses cease to till
He sees the flecks of flying foam
And dream-drifts, dapping down the drill

A railwayman lets by a train
Then leans across the stile and chats
A "Bubble" bobbing in his brain
His mind a maze of old, spent knats

For look! along Lough Erne's Shore
Old hawthorns in the christening shawls
Do beckon to the idle oar
And sun that squints through cloudy squalls

Round stones and rocks and stunted trees
The hunt for new-hatched fly begins
And dappers down upon their knees
Do penance for their tall-tale sins

The brown boat and it's crew of three
Are nosing from the point away
The eager oars dip fast and free
Then slow, she broad-sides up the bay

Where spindrift seethes with mayfly sap
A big one wallows like a whale
He rises to the stern dap
And takes it in a head-and-tail

"I'm in him, he's a mighty trout!"
The rod all a hoop, the racing reel
Grasshopper-ticks the blowline out
To bring the haughty fish to heel

The flush five-pounder's race is run
He lies gill-gasping on the floor
While light spoke-wheeling from the sun
Throws silver on the bladed oar

"I mind a day", Big Thomas told,
"When heading down the second drift
Twas rougher though and rather cold
With cloud that only showers shift

"When sudden, night fell on that noon
And inshore flew the frightened gull
And every sound of living June
Was stiffled in a leaden lull

"We bent upon the oars and strove
With a strength of ten in every stroke
To reach some sheltered, wooded shore
Before the fearful storm broke

"Like crack of doom the thunder smote
And lightening skivered down the sky
Round rocking bay and reeling boat
The main rake-shafted shoulder-high

"Though fast we baled as fast she filled
With blistered hands we wrought away
When all at once the storm stilled
But we were wet I needn't say!"

"You're in a fish! now hold him tight!"
"What weight?" "I'd say four pounds a-half
Or maybe more, he's full of fight
Throw down the net and grab that gaff!"

The songs of Scotland came easily across the seas of Moyle to the northern part of this island. In the Glens of Antrim, for instance, there were songs like the Glenshesk version of *The Mountain Streams* and even much further south, down in Ballygee near Belleek, I heard Phillip Breen's mother, God rest her, sing a version of *The Whinny Knowes.* No one can dispute that this is other than a Scottish song and a fine one to boot.

The old grá for the Stuarts never died in the hearts of the people in this country. They tell the story still in parts of Donegal that after Culloden, when Bonnie Prince Charlie was forced to go on his keeping, he was spirited over the sea and given sanctuary in the wild and lonely valley of Glencolumcill, in south-west Donegal.

He was much fatigued from his journeyings in disguise and slept for three days and nights in the shelter and safety of the Glen. Bean a' tí became perturbed, fearing that he might not waken at all, so she rushed to a neighbour's house and declared: "Tá sé in a chodladh anois agus níl an oiread Béarla 'sa teach a's a mhusclóidh é." (He is now asleep and there is not as much English in the house as will waken him!)

My mother had a healthy dislike for James, who ran away at the Battle of the Boyne, and invariably referred to him as Séamus a' Chaca, although she had no Irish. She dearly loved Charles Edward, the Young Pretender, and sang two melodious songs in his praise, as only she could sing them. The first was *Prince Charlie Stuart:*

161

Come join in la-menta-tion, ye princ-es and no-bles— and
kings of the high-est— de-gree And— pit-y the lot of a
poor for-lorn— mai-den— Who mourns for her love night and
day.— Al-though she's but a la-dy of eighty pounds a year, Both
lords, dukes and earls — to her they do draw near, She— dis-
tains them all with si-lence and she bids them dis ap-pear,
For so dear was my Char-lie to me.

If you had seen my Charlie at the head of his army
He was a pleasant sight to behold
With his fine, silken hose on his bonnie brown leg
And his buckles of the pure, shining gold
The tartan my love wore was of yellow and green silk
And his lovely skin in under it far whiter than the milk
It's no wonder there were hundreds of highlanders killed
In restoring my Charlie to me

O, my love was six feet two, without stocking or shoe,
In proportion my true love was built
As I told you before upon Culloden Moor
Where the brave highland army was kilt
Prince Charlie Stuart was my true lover's name
He was champion of Scotland and son to King James
And so far have they banished him over the main
And so dear was my Chrlie to me
But the grief and the sorrow that blights my to-morrow
Between and betwixt us does stand
That my Charlie was brought up in the Catholic Religion
And I in the Church of Scotland
But if that is all divides us, although my kin may mock
I will go with my Charlie and worship at a Rock
And I'll become a member of Saint Peter's flock
And so dear was my Charlie to me.

And then she would follow with *The Blackbird,* that most
beautiful of all Jacobite songs with a range that taxes the best
traditional singers.

There was another pleasant little song she had that would
seem to have come from Scotland also. She called it *Lovely
Annie* and I never heard it sung by any other. Here it is:

As I went a walk-ing are— morn-ing in — May
I — spied love-ly— An-nie a — mak-ing — the— hay, —
And as— she moved on-ward, the — grass on each side
Through a gap in— the bush-es my An-nie I spied.

I went to the North Highlands to work by the day
And when I returned she was married away
Though she swore to be constant both loyal and true
But now she has gone and left me, do! what will I do?

Far better transported, far better for aye,
My mind turns to madness since Annie's away
She was my first and false true-love, my treasure and store
O Annie, lovely Annie, will I e'er see you more?

Some people they tell me love has me led blind
My master he says that he'll have me confined
That he'll send me to Bedlam, bind me in strong chains
For your sake, lovely Annie, I suffer those pains

Come all you stout heroes, take a warning in time
And never trust a red rose or lily in prime
For the green leaves will wither, and the branches decay
And the roots they will torment you when the flowers fade away

Lone lisper in a legend land
With bridled tongue and broken sword
How hope to meet the bardic band
With borrowed Béarla at the Ford?

Gird on this breastplate, take that shield
That shines with light of learning old.
I'll bring you where the heart is healed
Of longing in the Land of Gold . . .

I answered the call and did as I was told. I reached the Promised Land but Oisín suddenly disappeared, and left me holding a mighty image by the mane. At length I managed to mount my steed and in time mastered him. He has brought me to many strange and wonderful places.

On one occasion we stopped with Kitty Gallagher of Middle Dore and she sang *Connlach Ghlas an Fhómhair,* a song that would warm the cockles of the coldest heart. I translated it into the other tongue and dedicated my version to my wife, Sheila.

Ar chonnlaigh ghlais an Fhómhair a stóirín gur dhearc mé uaim
Ba deas do chos i mbróig 'sba ró-dheas do leagan siúil
Do ghruaidh ar dhath   na rósaí's do chuirníní bhí fighte dlúith
Mo nuar gan sinn 'ár bpósadh nó'r bord luinge 'triall 'un siúil

Tá buachaillí na h-áite seo a' gartha 'gus ag éirí teann
Is lucht na gcocán ard a' déanamh fárais do mo chailín donn
Dá ngluaisfeadh Rí na Spáinne thar saile is a shlóite cruinn
Bhrúighfinn féar is fásach is bheinn ar láimh le mo chailín donn

Ceannach buaibh ar aonaigh dá mbeinn agus mo chailín donn
Gluais is tar a chéad-searc nó go dtéidh muid thar Ghaoth Bearra
       anonn
Go scartar ó na chéile barr na gcraobh agus an eala ó'n tuinn
Ní scarfar sinn ó chéile 's níl ach baos díbh a chur in bhur gceann

Sé chuala mé Dia Domhnaigh mar chómhrá 'gabháil eadar mnáibh
Go raibh sí 'gabháil á pósadh ar óighfhear dá bhfuil san áit
A stóirín, glac mo chomhairle 's a' fómhar seo fán mar tá
's chá leigim le 'bhfuil beo thú, a stór, nó is tú mo ghrá

My lasting love, my joy supreme, in autumn lean I looked from me
And found the wine of wisdom old in hazeled health on nutting-tree
Your features fair as any rose, your heels and hose old hags begrudge
My grief that we're not on the foam beyond their hate and
    elbow-nudge

The heroes of this haggard small wear shrunken eels on
    handstaff-head
Their buailtíns flash on old barn door, they shout and roar of bridal
    bed
But if the king of Holy Spain would smuggle grain and grapes once
    more
I'd spill their blood on stumps and sand and hold your hand for
    evermore

If I were with my wee brown girl beyond the span of Barra's oak
The buying and the selling men would twist their beards and long
    pipes smoke
Until they break asunder the top branch and the bridled broom
The wonder of such whitened flame would wave and swan
    in love consume

Last Sunday tidings came to me as gossips gabbled over cups
That my brown girl was going to wed with one who had more downs
    than ups
My darling take your love's advice and do not splice till Easter day
When we'll be safe beyond their sight and wicked spite
    far, far away

There's another little song I learned in Dublin from Hudie
Devenney of Ranafast many years ago. It goes like this:

AN SAIGHDIÚIR TRÉIGTHE
Nuair a d'éirigh mé maidin Dia Cheadaoin'
níor choisreac mé m' éadán faraor
Nó gur bheir mé ar an arm a ba ghéire
agus chuir mé a bhéal le cloich líomhth'
Caith mise domh mo chuid éadaigh
is mo chiall mhaith gur leig mé le gaoith
'S nuair a chuala mé iomradh 'r mo chéad-searc
Steall mé 'n corr-mhéar ó'n alt díom

Is fada mo chosa gan bhróga,
gus is faide mo phócaí gan phingin
Is fada mé 'gabháil le mná óga,
ach níor ól mé riamh deoch le mo mhian
Is fada mo chradh chroí-s' á dhéanamh
Mo thumba á prionntáil ag saor
'Gus mo chomhnair á tógáil lá'n Earraigh
'Gus na buachaillí deasa gabháil faoi

Dá mbeinn-se seacht mbliana faoi'n talamh
Ná i bhfiabhras na leabtha mo luí
A chéad-searc dá dtiocfá 'gus m'fiafraighe
Scéal cinnte go mbeinn leat mo shuí
Is trua nach marbh bhí m' athair
Nuair a chuir sé mé go h-arm a' ríogh
'Sgurbh í'n uaigh mo chruadh-leabaidh feasta
's a chéad-searc nach trua leat mo luí

THE FORSAKEN SOLDIER
When I rose like a Russian that morning
No cross on my forehead I signed
For the thought that my true-love had left me
It drove me clean out of mind
I reached for a scythe that hung high in the hawthorn
Fell to her with file and a blue sharping-stone
And stripped to the waist in the cornfield
I cut half the harvest alone

My feet are too long without leather
My pockets much longer want gold
I envy the old mountain wether
For his love tales need never be told
They say that this heartache all winter will tarry
And lead to the tomb before next Easter day
And the boys that I hurled with will carry
My corpse to it's rest in the clay

If I were stretched prone with the fever
Or seven years under the ground
And you came to my tomb love and called me
I would rise from the dead with one bound
My sorrow that death didn't strike down my father
'Fore he drove me to drink and the king's own armie
In the boneyard my hard bed is waiting
O my darling have pity on me!

According Breandán Ó Buachalla, a scholar and man
of learning, Cathal Buí Mac Giolla Gunna, the Ulster poet
and wanderer, was born in County Fermanagh in 1680, some
ten years before the Battle of the Boyne. Be this as it may, I
am proud to claim him as a son of the Lough Shore and it is
interesting to note that he predeceased Denis McCabe, Caldwell's musician and jester, by only fourteen years.

Perhaps they met. Whether they did or not they would
have had a lot in common. Unquestionably Cathal's best
known poem and song is *An Bunnán Buí*. This song is known
throughout the nine counties of Ulster and indeed also in the
province of Connacht. It is a exquisite song of self-mockery
and was absorbed into the mainstream of traditional Gaelic
song. Anonymous verses were added from time in various
Gaeltacht areas. Here is my own translation of it.

'Twas break of day but no bittern's horn
Filled the waking morn with it's hollow boom
For I found him prone on a bare flag blown
By the loughshore lone where he met his doom
His legs were sunk in the slime and slunk
A hostage held in the fangs of frost
O men of knowledge lament his going
For want of liquor his life was lost

O yellow bird, tis my bitter grief
I'd as lee or lief that my race was run
No hunger's tooth but a parching drouth
That has sapped your youth after all your fun
Far worse to me than the Sack of Troy
That my darling boy with the frost was slain
No want or woe did his wings bestow
As he drank the flow of a brown bog drain

Degrading vile was the way you died
My bittern beauteous of glowing sheen
'Twas at dawn each day that your pipe you'd play
As content you lay on a hillock green
O my great fatigue and my sorrow sore
That your tail is higher than heart or head
And the tipplers say as they pass this way
Had he drunk his fill he would not be dead

O bittern bright 'tis my thousand woes
That the rooks and crows are all pleasure bound
With the rats and mice as they cross the ice
To indulge in vice at your funeral mound
Had word reached me of your woeful plight
On the ice I'd smite and the water free
You'd have all that lake for the thirst to slake
And we'd hold no wake for the Bunnán Buí

'Tis not the blackbird that I'm bewailing
Or thrush assailing the blossomed braes
But my bittern yellow, that hearty fellow
Who has got my hue and my willful ways
By the loughshore bank he forever drank
And his sorrow sank in the rolling wave
Come sun or rain every drop I'll drain
For the cellar's empty beyond the grave

If any poet had his finger on the pulse of the people it was Cathal Buí. No Irish writer before or since has translated the great heart cry of the inarticulate masses into language so poignant and compelling. Take for instance his beautiful love song, *Cáitlín Triail, Kitty Tyrell.* We can feel the frost of infidelity along with that of winter knawing into his very vitals.

That he was hounded and harrassed by the clergy of his day is of little import. The man who could write a repentance poem like *Aithreachas Chathail Bhuí,* as he lay dying in a lonely bothóg, remote from friends and companions, could not be left long outside the Gates of Heaven.

His was a healthy wholesome existence and if he drowned his drouth in the juice of the barley who are we to blame him? The poet who most resembles Cathal Buí as a writer in the idiom of the people today is unquestionably the mighty Patrick Kavanagh himself.

Did destiny ordain that the last resting-place of Kavanagh, the poet of the Great Hunger, should be so close to that of Mac Giolla Gunna, the poet of the Great Thirst? One poet lies in Inniskeen and the other in Donaghmoyne; singers who so wonderfully wove the weft of their muse with the warp of the people.

And now to conclude and to finish my journey, I give you a song beloved of the gentle and genial Joe Holmes, a troubadour from North Antrim, who went to God early in 1978. May the sod lie lightly on his bones!

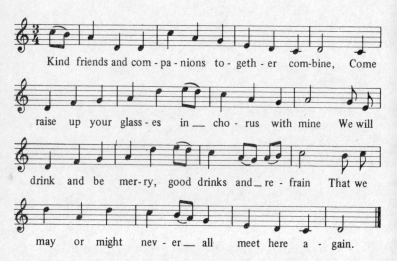

Kind friends and com-pa-nions to-geth-er com-bine, Come raise up your glass-es in — cho-rus with mine We will drink and be mer-ry, good drinks and — re-frain That we may or might nev-er — all meet here a - gain.

Chorus:
Here's a health to the company, and one to my lass
We will drink and be marry all out of one glass
We will drink and be merry, good drinks and refrain
That we may or might never all meet here again.

Here's a health to the wee lass that I love so well
For style or for beauty there's none can excel
She smiles on my countenance as she sits on my knee
There is none in this wide world so happy as me. *Chorus*

Our ship lies at anchor and ready to dock
I wish her safe landing without shake or shock
And when we are sailing to the land of the free
I will always remember your kindness to me. *Chorus*

I have read that old proverb, I have read it so true
My love she's as far as the bright morning dew
I have read that old proverb, I suppose so have you
So good friends and companions I bid you adieu. *Chorus*

Alts *Cliffs*

bacán-bound *tethered*
barrem *the wash for a still*
bedtick *mattress*
besom *broom*
black forty seven *1847, the famine year*
B-men *N.I. special police*
bodach *boor*
bogged *stuck*
bonive *a little pig/piglet*
booragh *a home made rope*
bowran (bodhrán) *a one-sided drum*
brae-face *hillside*
brashes *spells of work*
bruagh *bank*
bothóg *a sod cabin*

Cailleach Béara *The Hag of Béara*
cantman *pedlar*
caoineadh *keening*
cat breacs *Gaelic-speaking proselytisers*
ceapair *a buttered slice of bread*
ceaped *stopped*
céilí, making a, *visiting*
chincough *whooping cough*
cologing *conversing*
Conor Mac Neasa *a High King of Ireland*
cope-carlied *capsized*
coped *turned lea sods*
crathán *final touch*
creel *rod basket for holding turf*
crigs *sound made by hobnails on flagstones*
Crom Cruaidh *Celtic God*

crubach cows *worthless cows*
cuinneog *a blade of grass*

dam *waterhole where flax is steeped*
doughty *tough*
drouth *thirst*
dudeen *clay pipe*

féar gortach *hungry grass*

garner *harvest*
garsún *boy*
glais gaibhlinn *magic cow*
gleed *a spark*
grá *love*
grandeer buck magpie *nonsense rhyme*
greeshagh *ashes and cinders in which live coals are raked on open hearth*
gudgel *axle of wheelbarrow*
gulder *shout or raucous roar*

haggard *stack-yard*
headsheaf *top sheaf or finishing touch*
holic-colic *belly ache*

in the rere *at the latter end*

jibble *to churn*
join *collect money for purchase of drink*
jundy *jostle*

Keeby knowes *rough, hilly land*
kilty *one distilled 'wash' in poteen making*
kittling *kitten*
knuckle a knee *kneel*

laghey *civil*
lea *new broken land*
a lock *a little or a few*

meelamurder *a riot or row*
meitheal *co-operative team of workers*

mern ditch *boundary fence*
moider *confuse*
mórtas cine *pride of race*

paltog *hell-for-leather*
pavers *hob-nailed boots*
piggin *measure*
pritties *potatoes*
putty leggings *cloth-legging worn by soliders*

ranns *verses*
raparee *highway man*
Red Branch Knights *The Knights of Eamhain Macha*
ribbonman *member of a resistance movement*
rickling *an unstable structure*
rime *a deposit of mist*
ris *enraged*
roof couple *wooden coupling support for roof*
roof scraws *sods on roof*
running a heat *distillation of poteen*

saggin *reed*
sally bushes *willows*
sceilp *sliver*
scollops *pointed rods used for thatching*
screak *dawn*
scutched *process in flax working*
sevendably *seven doubles; excessively*
shanks mare *on foot or walking*
shaughran, went clear a, *went astray*
sheeg *large round stack of hay*
shinned *climbed*
shough *drain*
skew *concrete protection between thatch and gable*
slunging *to drive cattle forcefully with a stick*
slunks *quagmires*
spar *an area of thatch*
spéirbhean *beautiful woman*
splanks *sparks*

sprigging *needlework*
spun the yarn *told a tale*
squireen *small squire*
stappling *stuffing of thatch into a roof cavity*
stirabout *porridge*
stirks *two-year-old cattle*
stook *a structure of sheaves*
strillions *streamers or bunting*
styme *nothing*
swain *love-lorn fellow*
swallow-tail *style of coat*
swither *indecisive*

tatty-hokers *potato harvesters*
thole *put-up with*
toe-plates *steel-tips on toes of hobnails*
traun *contrary*
trepan *torture*
trig *tidy*
troth *truth*
turnip-tailers *turnip harvesters*
turnip-toppers *turnip harvesters*

wag *wit*
weechels *small children*
weemin *women*
wether *a castrated male sheep*
whangs *leather laces*
whetstone *grindstone*
whottling *sound made by duck with its beak in a puddle*
worm *copper pipe used in poteen distillation*

INDEX OF SONGS AND POEMS
Words and music are given for songs marked*

177